E S T A T E   P U B L

G000168160

FAREHAM - G(

SARISBURY · WARSASH · TITC........ ...
PORTCHESTER · STUBBINGTON · LEE-ON-SOLENT

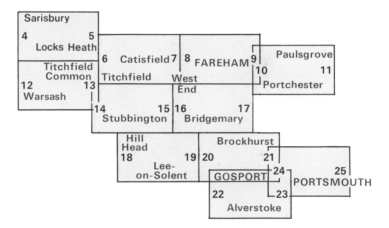

ROAD MAP pages 2–3
INDEX TO STREETS page 26

Every effort has been made to verify the accuracy of information in this book but the publishers cannot accept responsibility for expense or loss caused by any error or omission. Information that will be of assistance to the user of the maps will be welcomed.

The representation of a road, track or footpath on the maps in this atlas is no evidence of the existence of a right of way.

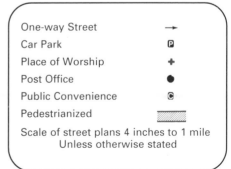

One-way Street →

Car Park P

Place of Worship +

Post Office ●

Public Convenience ⊙

Pedestrianized

Scale of street plans 4 inches to 1 mile
Unless otherwise stated

Street plans prepared and published by ESTATE PUBLICATIONS, Bridewell House, TENTERDEN, KENT, and based upon the ORDNANCE SURVEY maps with the sanction of the Controller of H. M. Stationery Office.

The publishers acknowledge the co-operation of Fareham and Gosport District Councils in the preparation of these maps.

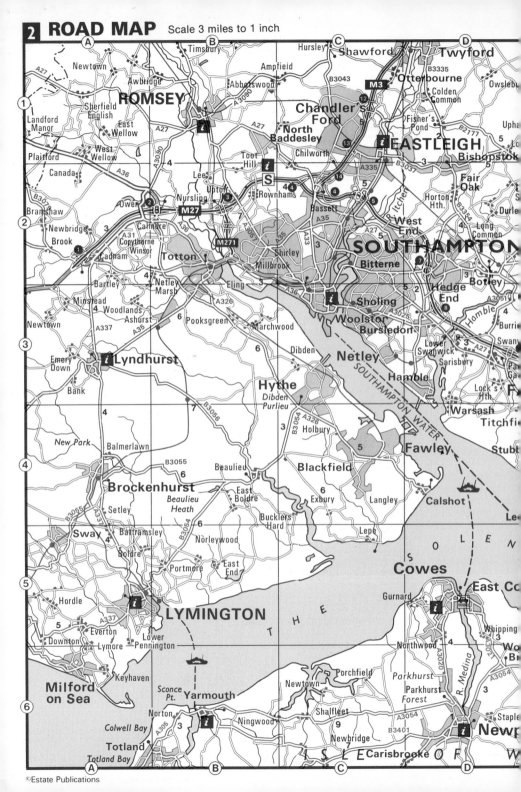

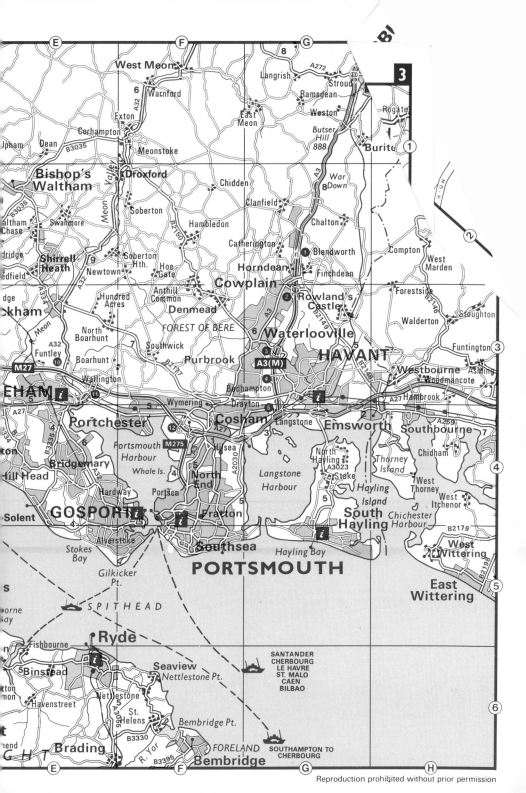

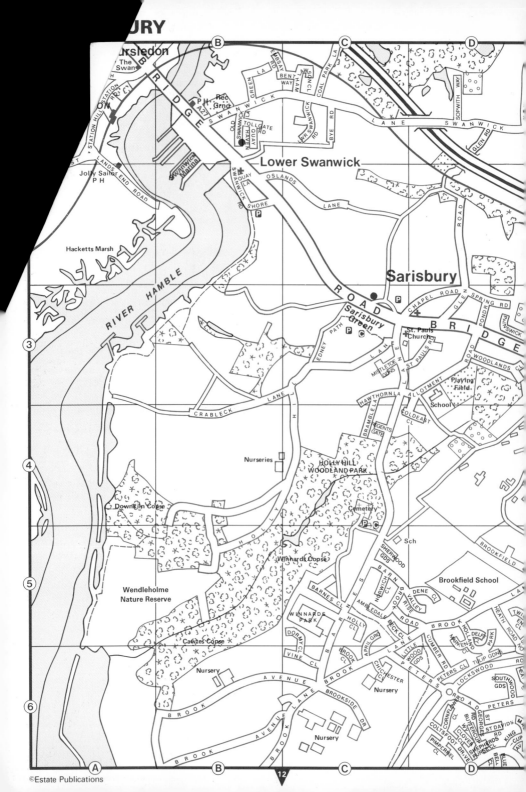

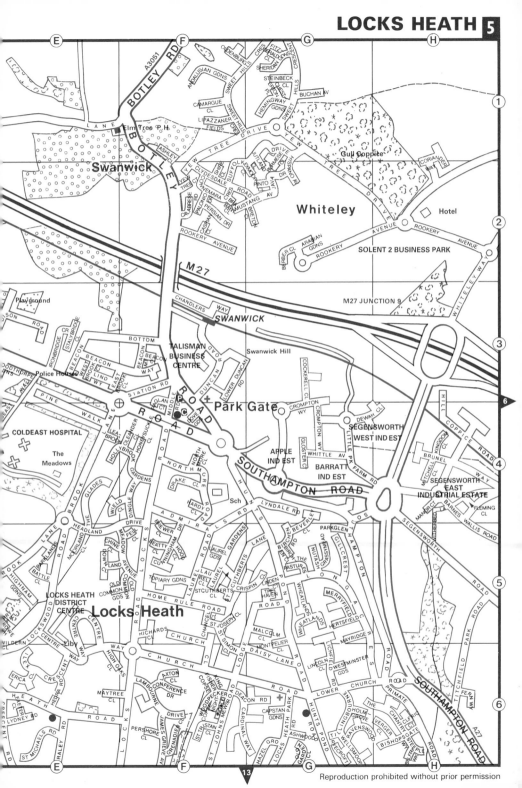

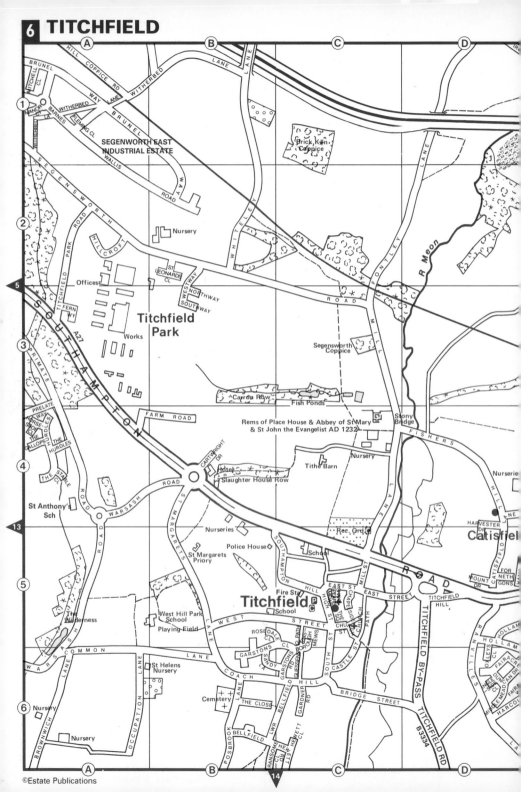

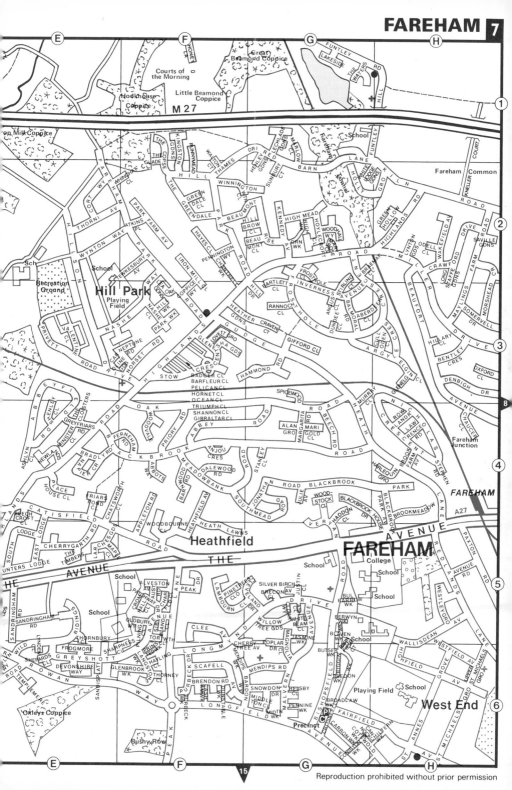

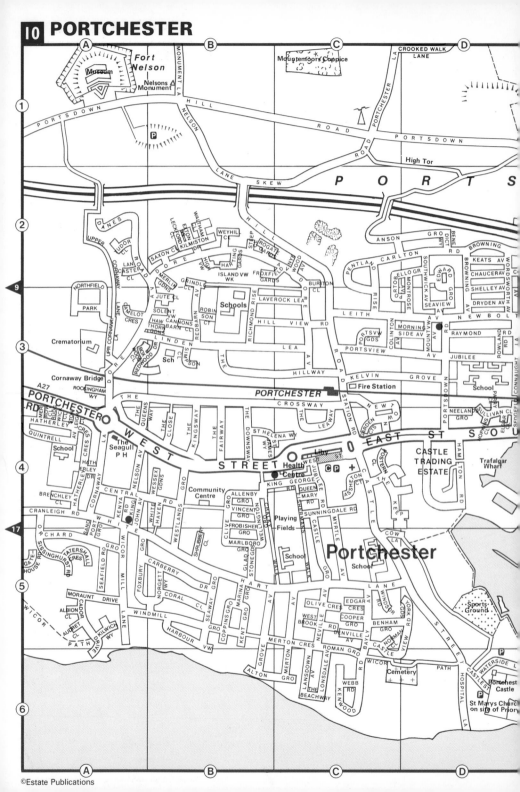

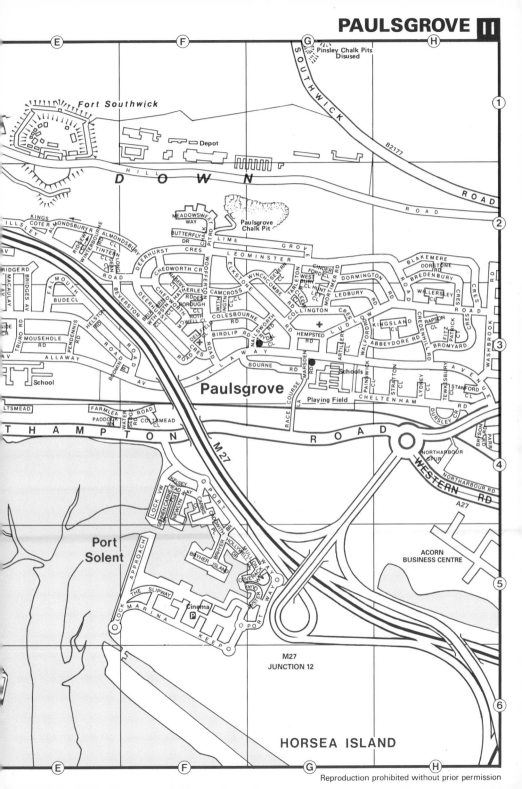

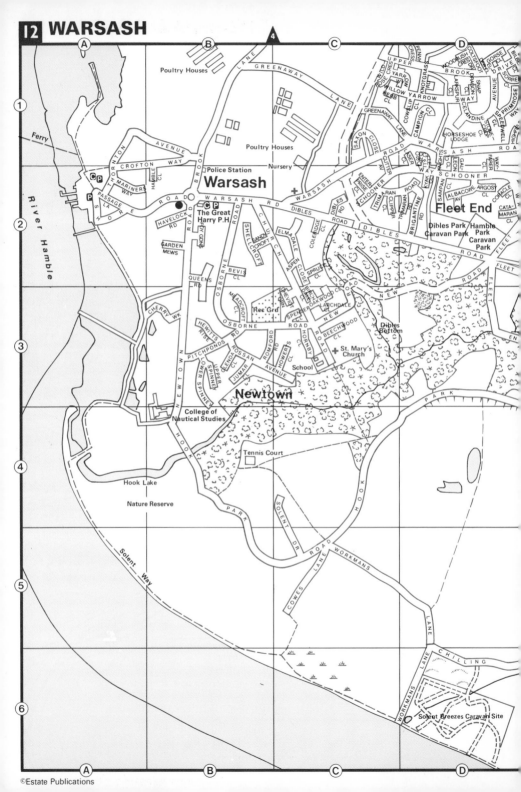

Titchfield Common

St Anthony's Sch

School

Abshot Manor
Country Club

Abshot House
Squash Club

Abshot

Household Waste
Amenity Point

Hook

Hookhead
Coppice

Hookgate Coppice

Nursery

Nursery

Holmepond
Row

The
Wilderness

Recn. Grd.

Chilling

Chilling Copse

North Heath
Coppice

Chilling Moor
Coppice

Brownwich
Pond

Thatchers Coppice

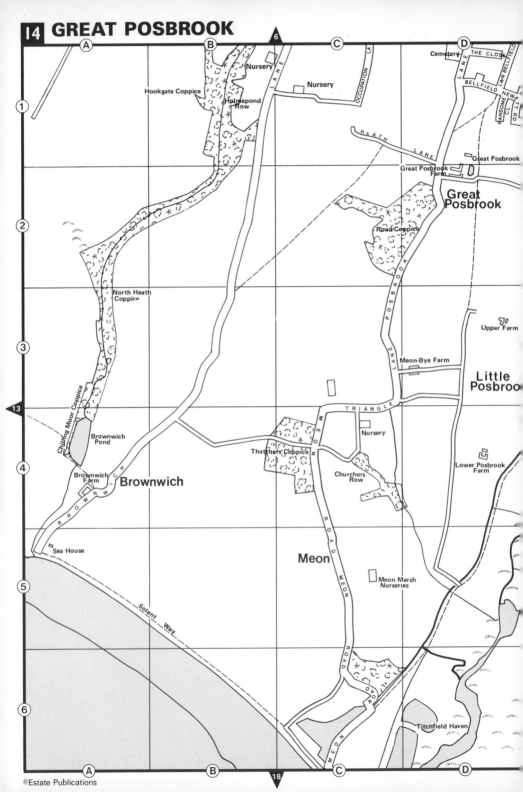

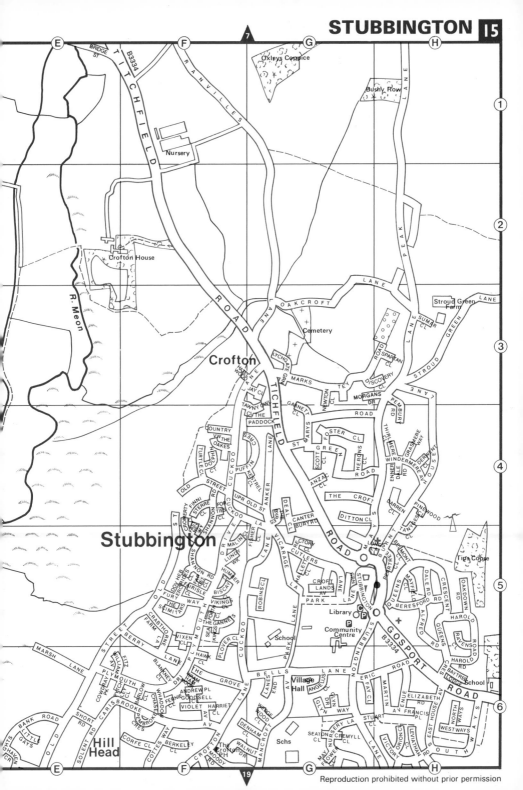

E   F   9   G   H

South Park

Cunigre Pond

GOLF
COURSE

Salterns
Quay

Sports Ground

CRANLEIGH RD

Wicor Marsh

Wicor Lake

Cams
Salt Marsh

Fareham Lake

Heavy Reach

Foxbury Point

ctory

Fleetlands

Depot

LEDERLE LANE

Bedenham

PRIMROSE
CL
BRIDGEMARY
WAY
BRIDGEMARY
GRO

RNAY
FLEETLANDS

FOXBURY LANE

FOXBURY LA

F E A R E H A M

PRIDEAUX-
BRUNE

NORTHWAY
AV
FRASER
RD

GREGSON
AV

HASLEMERE
AV

BATTEN
AV

SOUTHWAY

GREGSON
AV

THE
LEISURE
CL

CUNNINGHAM
DR

AERODROME
ROAD

BEDENHAM
LANE

HARWOOD
CL

VIAN CL
GDS

HORTON
MONTGOMERY
RD

SOUTHWAY

HARRIS RD

Bridgemary

KEYES
CL
CAMERON
CL
AGNEW
RD

Rec
Gnd

White
Horse
Inn

School

Schools

North Star
P.H.

PORTAL
RD

LAYTON
RD
FISHER
RD

BRIDGEMARY
AVENUE

TEDDER
RD

NAVELL
RD

TARN
RD

Frater
Lake

Elson Wood

School

PERTH
ROAD

CAMP
ROAD
CLO

BALMORAL
RD

BRAEMAR
RD

BEVERLY
LANE

Fort
Elson

Schools

Community
Centre

Library

BREWERS
LANE

BRAEMAR
CL

LERRYN
RD

NOBLE
CL

Bridgemary
Arch

DOWNSIDE
WAY

RNAD FRATER

GUNNERS
WAY

Wych
Way Inn

BIRCH
CL

RAMSAY
PL

HOLLY
CL

HAWKINS
WAY

FOUNDRY
WAY

TICHBORNE
WAY

FORTON
WAY

SAVERNAKE
CL

KEDERS
PL

CHARNWOOD

Holbrook

ROWNER
LANE

BEAUCHAMP
AV

JACOMB
PL

STOCK
LER PL

ORANGE
GRO

YEW

R O A D
A32

E   F   21   G   H

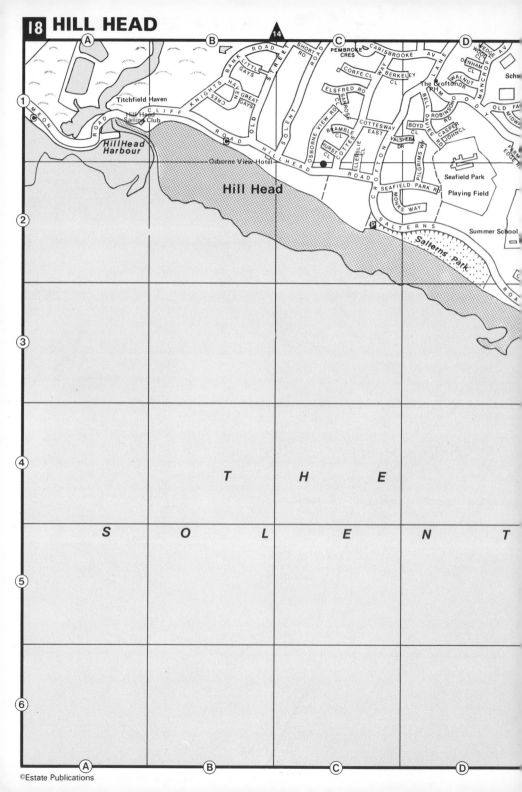

Titchfield Haven

Hill Head Sailing Club

HillHead Harbour

Osborne View Hotel

Hill Head

PEMBROKE CRES

CARISBROOKE

CORFE CL

BERKELEY CL

The Crofton RH

WALNUT

DENHAM

WEDGE WOOD CL

WOOL AV

MANCROFT

Schs

Old Fa

MIDWAY

ELSFRED RD

COTTESWAY EAST

BRAMBLE CL

BOYD CL

ROBINSON RD

CASPER

JOHN CL

BELL DAVIES RD

VALSHEBA DR

SHORT RD

ROAD

STREET

SOLENT

OSBORNE VIEW RD

HURST CL

ELLERSLIE CL

SEAFIELD PARK RD

CROFTON

PILGRIMS WY

MONTS WAY

Seafield Park

Playing Field

Summer School

SALTERNS

Salterns Park

ROAD

P

BANK

LITTLE GAYS

GREAT GAYS

HALF GAYS

CRES

KNIGHTS

CLIFF

ROAD

OLD

HILLHEAD

ROAD

MEON

ROAD

THE

SOLENT

©Estate Publications

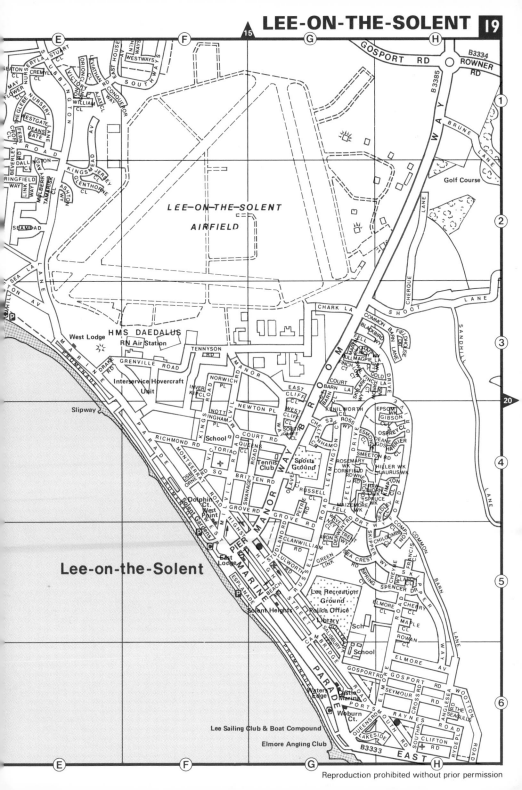

Lee-on-the-Solent

LEE-ON-THE-SOLENT AIRFIELD

HMS DAEDALUS
RN Air Station

GOSPORT RD
ROWNER RD

Golf Course

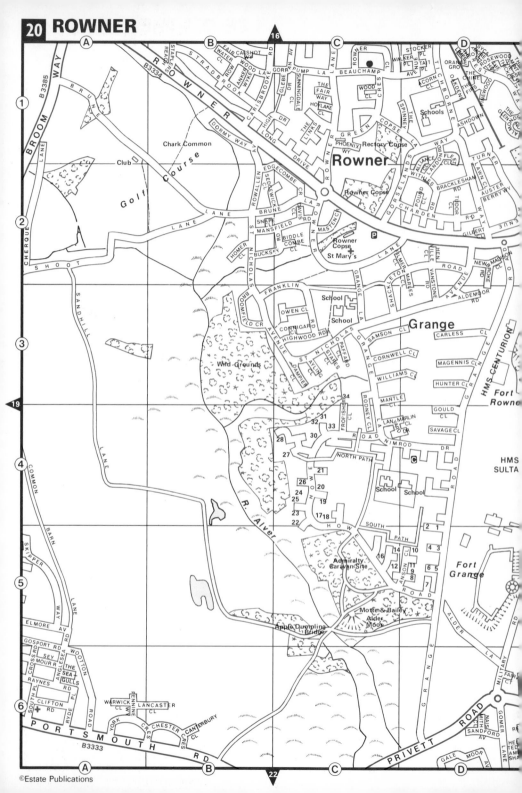

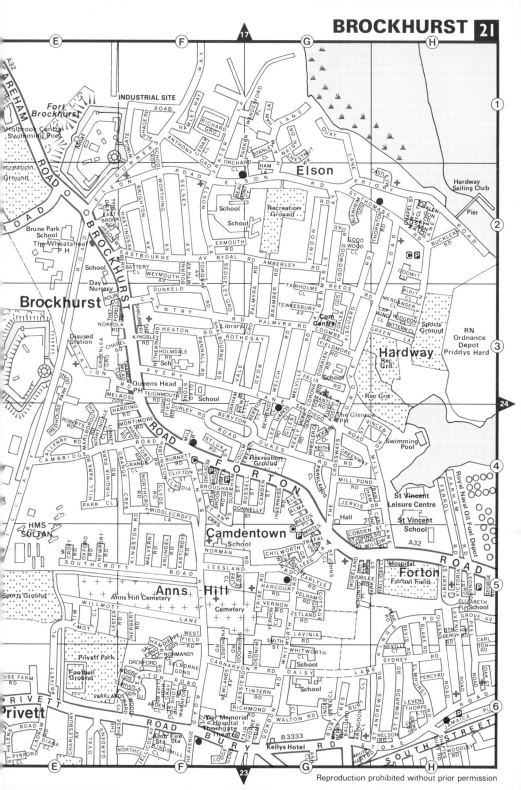

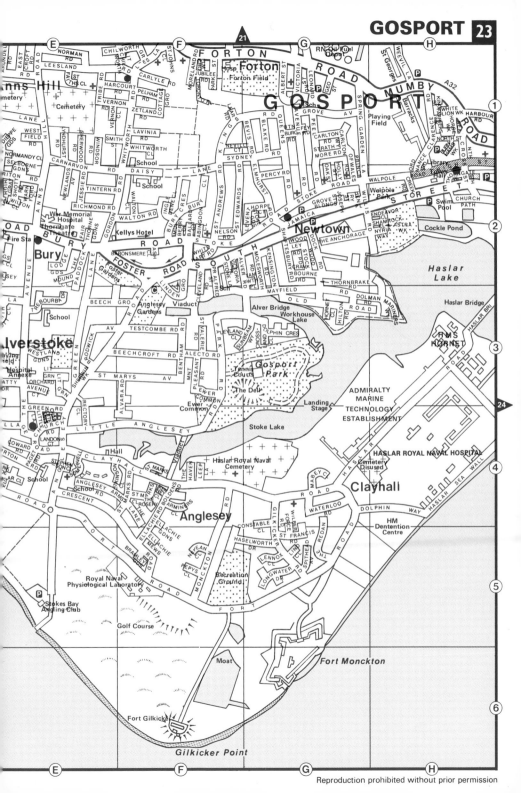

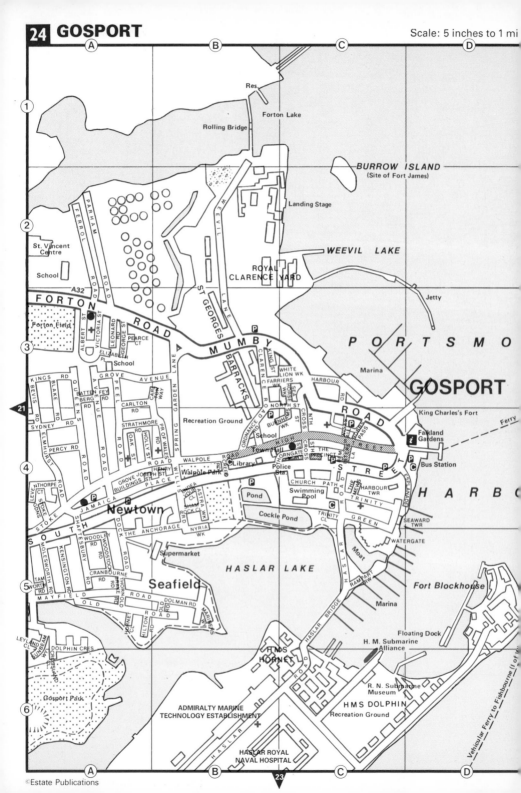

Res.

Forton Lake

Rolling Bridge

BURROW ISLAND
(Site of Fort James)

Landing Stage

St. Vincent
Centre

School

WEEVIL LAKE

Jetty

A32

FORTON ROAD

Forton Field

ROYAL
CLARENCE YARD

PORTSMO

PARHAM ROAD

FERROL ROAD

ST GEORGES LANE

WEEVIL LANE

MUMBY ROAD

Marina

GOSPORT

King Charles's Fort

Ferry

ALBERT ST

VICTORIA ST

LEONARD ST

GEORGE ST

PEARCE CT

ELIZABETH PL

School

KINGS LA

CLARENCE RD

WHITE LION WK

FARRIERS WK

HARBOUR

Falkland
Gardens

Bus Station

KINGS RD

BLAKE RD

QUEENS RD

GROVE AVENUE

PEEL RD

CARLTON RD

SPRING GARDEN LANE

ORDNANCE RD

NORTH ST

NTH CROSS ST

STH CROSS ST

HARBOUR RD

THE PRECINCT

HIGH STREET

ESPLANADE

Recreation Ground

HARBO

BEVIS

BATTEN FEY

BERG RD

PENZANCE

STRATHMORE RD

HOLLY RD

OAK ST

PO WALES

School

BUSH WK

THORNGATE

Town Hall

THE MEWS

Harbour
TWR

TRINITY

HARBOUR

SYDNEY RD

ELMHURST

PERCY RD

GROVE JOSEPH
Buildings

HENRY ST

Walpole Park

WALPOLE RD

Library

Police
Sta.

CHURCH PATH

Church

Swimming
Pool

TRINITY CL

TRINITY
GREEN

SEAWARD
TWR

WATERGATE

NTHORPE CT

STOKE RD

LEVE SONS RD

JAMAICA PL

Newtown

GROVE RD

DOCK RD

THE ANCHORAGE

CAMBER CL

ASTRA WK

SHAM ROCK WK

NYRIA WK

Pond

Cockle Pond

HASLAR RD

RAMPART ROW

Moat

Fort Blockhouse

SOUTH ST

SHAFTESBURY RD

WOODLEY RD

WOODSTOCK RD

Supermarket

HASLAR LAKE

Marina

MOLESWORTH RD

KENSINGTON RD

CRANBOURNE RD

THORNOLD RD

Seafield

DOLMAN RD

Floating Dock

H. M. Submarine
Alliance

TAM WORTH RD

MAYFIELD RD

OLD ROAD

HORNET RD

FILTON RD

MARINE RD

HASLAR BRIDGE ROAD

R. N. Submarine
Museum

HMS DOLPHIN
Recreation Ground

LEYLAND CL

DUNBAR

DORRISSIA

CRISSHAM

DOLPHIN CRES

Gosport Park

HMS
HORNET

ADMIRALTY MARINE
TECHNOLOGY ESTABLISHMENT

HASLAR

HASLAR ROYAL
NAVAL HOSPITAL

Vehicular Ferry to Fishbourne (I. of W.)

23

21

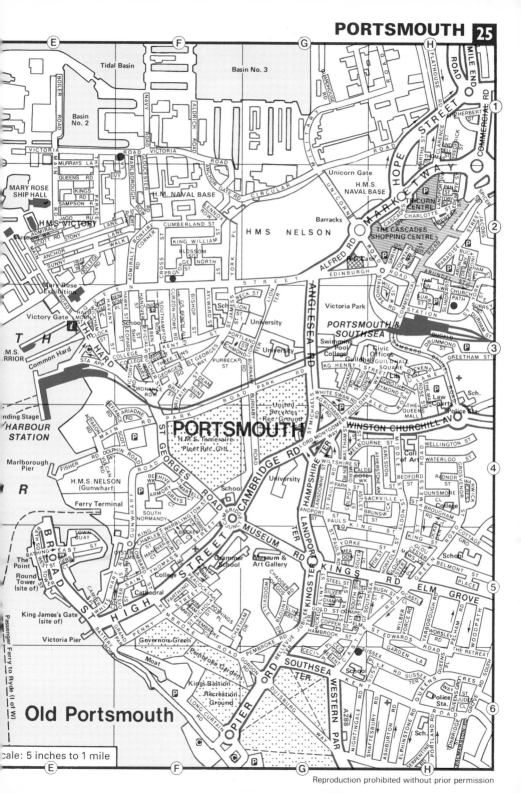

Scale: 5 inches to 1 mile

A - Z INDEX TO STREETS
with Postcodes

The Index includes some names for which there is insufficient space on the maps. These names are preceded by an * and are followed by the nearest adjoining thoroughfare.

Abbey Rd. PO15	7 F4	Arminers Clo. PO12	23 F4	Beechwood Clo. SO31	12 C3
Abbeydore Rd. PO6	11 H3	Armory La. PO1	25 F4	Beehive Walk. PO1	25 F4
Abbeyfield Dri. PO15	7 E4	Artillery Clo. PO6	11 G3	Behrendt Clo. PO12	21 G4
Abbots Way. PO15	7 F4	Arundel Dri. PO16	8 A4	Belfry Walk. SO31	5 H6
A'Becket Ct. PO1	25 F5	Arundel Rd. PO12	21 F5	Bell Davies Rd. PO14	18 D1
Aberdeen Clo. PO12	23 F2	Arundel St. PO1	25 H2	Bellevue Ter. PO5	25 G6
Abingdon Clo. PO15	7 G3	Arundel Way. PO1	25 H2	Bellfield. PO14	6 B6
Abshot Clo. PO14	13 F2	Ascot Clo. PO14	13 H1	Bells La. PO1	15 G6
Abshot Rd. PO14	13 F2	Ash Burton Rd. PO12	22 D4	Belmont Clo. PO14	15 H5
Acorn Clo. PO13	20 D1	Ash Clo. PO14	7 G5	Belmont Pl. PO5	25 H5
Actaeon Rd. PO1	25 E4	Ash Clo. PO12	23 F2	Belmont St. PO5	25 H5
Addison Rd. SO31	5 E3	Ashburton Rd. PO5	25 H6	Belvoir Clo. PO14	8 B5
Adelaide Pl. PO16	8 C5	Ashdown. PO13	20 D1	Bemisters La. PO12	24 C4
Admirals Rd. SO31	5 F4	Ashley Clo. SO31	5 F1	Benbow Pl. PO1	25 F3
Admirals Walk. PO1	25 E2	Ashley Ct. PO12	21 G5	Benedict Way. PO16	10 D2
Admirals Walk. PO12	22 D2	Ashlyn Clo. PO15	7 E4	Beneficial St. PO1	25 F3
Admiralty Rd. PO1	25 F2	Ashstead Clo. PO16	9 G5	Benham Gro. PO16	10 C5
Adur Rd. PO12	21 E3	Ashton Way. PO14	19 E2	Bentham Rd. PO13	23 F3
Aerodrome Rd. PO13	17 F4	Ashwood. SO31	5 G6	Bentham Way. SO31	4 C1
Agnew Rd. PO13	17 E5	Aspen Av. SO31	12 C2	Bentley Cres. PO16	7 H3
Ajax Clo. PO14	19 E1	Aspen Gro. PO12	20 D1	Berber Clo. PO15	5 G2
Alan Gro. PO15	7 F3	Assheton Ct. PO16	10 C4	Beresford Rd. PO14	15 H5
Albacore Av. SO31	12 D2	Astley St. PO5	25 G4	Berewood Clo. PO14	18 C1
Albatross Walk. PO13	16 D6	Astra Walk. PO12	24 B4	*Berkeley Ct,	
Albemarle Av. PO12	21 G3	Atherstone Walk. PO5	25 H4	Elmore Rd. PO13	19 H6
Albert Rd. PO14	16 C6	Atkins Pl. PO15	7 F2	Berry La. PO14	15 F5
Albert St. PO12	23 G1	Atkinson Clo. PO12	23 E4	Berwyn Walk. PO14	7 G5
Albion Clo. PO16	10 A5	Audret Clo. PO16	10 A6	Beryl Av. PO12	21 F2
Aldemoor Rd. PO13	20 D3	Aust Rd. PO14	7 F5	Beryton Clo. PO12	21 G4
Alder La. PO13	20 D5	Austerberry Way. PO13	20 D2	Beryton Rd. PO12	21 F4
Alders Rd. PO16	16 D1	Avenue Ct. PO12	23 E3	Beverley Clo. SO31	5 G5
Aldrich Rd. PO1	25 F1	Avenue Rd. PO14	8 A5	Beverley Rd. PO14	19 E2
Alec Rose La. PO1	25 H3	Avenue Rd. PO12	23 G1	Beverly Clo. PO13	17 F6
Alecto Rd. PO12	23 F3	Avery La. PO12	21 F3	Beverston Rd. PO6	11 E3
Alencon Clo. PO12	21 H2	Avocet Walk. PO13	16 C6	Bevis Clo. SO31	12 B2
Alex St. PO12	21 G4	Avon Clo. PO13	19 G5	Bevis Rd. PO12	23 G1
Alexander Gro. PO16	8 B6	Avon Wk. PO16	9 G5	Biddlecombe Clo. PO13	20 C2
Alfred Rd. PO14	15 H6	Ayling Clo. PO13	20 C3	Biggin Walk. PO14	7 G6
Alfred Rd. PO14	16 C6	Aylward St. PO1	25 F3	Bilberry Clo. SO31	12 D1
Allaway Av. PO6	11 E3			Birch Dri. PO13	17 E4
Allenby Gro. PO16	10 B4	Badger Clo. PO15	7 F3	Birchdale Clo. SO31	12 C3
Allenby Rd. PO12	21 E4	Ballard Ct. PO12	23 F2	Birchen Clo. SO31	5 G5
Alliance Clo. PO13	20 D2	Balliol Clo. PO14	13 G2	Birchen Rd. SO31	5 G5
Allotment Rd. SO31	4 D3	Balmoral Clo. PO13	17 F5	Birchmore Clo. PO13	17 E6
Alma St. PO12	21 G4	Balmoral Clo. PO15	7 G3	Birdlip Rd. PO6	11 F3
Almondsbury Clo. PO6	11 E2	Bankside. PO12	23 E4	Birdwood Gro. PO16	9 F5
Almondsbury Rd. PO6	11 E2	Bardon Way. PO14	7 G6	Biscay Clo. PO14	15 F5
Almondside. PO13	20 D1	Barfleur Clo. PO15	7 F3	Bishop St. PO1	25 F3
Alphage Rd. PO12	21 F1	Barham Clo. PO12	21 G4	Bishopsfield Rd. PO14	7 G6
Alton Gro. PO16	10 B6	Barlow Clo. PO14	15 F6	Bishopsgate. PO14	5 H6
Alum Way. PO16	9 E5	Barn Brook Rd. SO31	4 C5	Bittern Clo. PO12	21 H3
Alvara Rd. PO12	23 F3	Barnes Clo. SO31	4 C5	Blackbird Way. PO13	19 H3
Alver Rd. PO12	23 F2	Barnes La. SO31	4 C6	Blackbrook House Dri. PO14	7 G4
Alvercliffe Dri. PO12	22 D4	Barnes Wallis La. PO15	5 H4	Blackbrook Park. PO14	7 G4
Alveston Av. PO14	7 F5	Barnfield Clo. PO14	7 G6	Blackbrook Park Av. PO15	7 H4
Amberley Rd. PO12	21 G2	Barnwood Rd. PO15	7 F4	Blackbrook Rd. PO15	7 E4
Ambledale. SO31	4 C5	Baronsmere. PO12	23 E2	Blakemere Cres. PO6	11 H2
Amersham Clo. PO12	22 C2	Barratt Ind Est. SO31	5 G4	Blake Rd. PO12	23 G1
Anchor Gate Rd. PO1	25 F2	Bartlett Clo. PO15	7 G3	Blankney Clo. PO14	15 F6
Anchor La. PO1	25 E2	Bath La. PO16	8 C5	Blaven Walk. PO14	7 G5
Andalusian Gdns. PO15	5 F1	Bath Sq. PO1	25 E5	Blenheim Gdns. PO12	21 G2
Andrew Bell St. PO1	25 H1	Bathing La. PO1	25 E5	Blossom Sq. PO1	25 F2
Andrew Pl. PO14	15 F6	Battenberg Rd. PO12	24 A3	Blount Rd. PO1	25 G5
Angelus Clo. PO14	15 G6	Battery Clo. PO12	21 F2	Bluebell Clo. SO31	4 D6
Anglesea Rd. PO12	23 E4	Battery Row. PO1	25 E5	Boarhunt Rd. PO17	9 E2
Anglesea Rd. PO13	19 H6	Battle Clo. SO31	5 E5	Bodmin Rd. PO6	11 E3
Anglesea Rd. PO1	25 G3	Bay Rd. PO12	22 D3	Boiler Rd. PO1	25 E1
Anglesey Arms Rd. PO12	23 E4	Bayly Av. PO16	10 C5	Boldens Rd. PO12	23 F4
Angus Clo. PO15	7 G3	Baytree Lodge. PO14	15 H6	Bonfire Corner. PO1	25 F2
Anjou Cres. PO15	7 F4	Beach Rd. PO13	19 G5	Bosham Walk. PO13	16 D6
Anker La. PO14	15 G4	Beacon Bottom. SO31	5 E3	Botley Rd. SO19	5 F1
Anker Wyke. PO13	20 B1	Beacon Clo. SO31	5 F3	Bourne Rd. PO6	11 G3
Anns Hill Rd. PO12	21 F4	Beacon Mnt. SO31	5 F3	Bournemouth Av. PO14	21 F2
Anson Rd. PO13	20 D5	Beacon Way. SO31	5 E3	Boxwood Clo. PO16	10 A3
Anson Gro. PO16	10 C2	Beaconsfield Rd. PO16	8 B6	Boyd Clo. PO14	18 D1
Anthony Gro. PO12	21 F1	Beatty Clo. SO31	5 F5	Boyd Rd. PO13	16 D4
Anzac Clo. PO14	15 G4	Beatty Dri. PO12	23 E3	Brabant Clo. PO15	5 F2
Apple Ind Est. SO31	5 G4	Beauchamp Av. PO13	20 C1	Bracklesham Rd. PO13	20 D2
Appleton Rd. PO15	7 F5	Beaufort Av. PO16	7 H3	Brading Av. PO13	17 E6
April Gro. SO31	4 C6	Beaulieu Av. PO16	9 G5	Bradly Rd. PO15	7 F6
Arabian Gdns. PO15	5 G2	Beaulieu Pl. PO13	16 D6	Braemar Clo. PO13	17 F6
Archery La. PO16	8 C4	Beaumont Clo. PO15	7 G2	Braemar Clo PO15	7 G2
Arden Clo. PO12	21 F6	Beaumont Ct. PO12	21 F2	Braemar Rd PO13	17 F5
Argosy Clo. SO31	12 D2	Beaumont Rise. PO15	7 F2	Bramber Rd. PO12	21 G3
Argyle Cres. PO15	7 H3	Beck Clo. PO14	4 C5	Bramble Clo. PO14	18 C1
Ariadne Rd. PO1	25 F4	Beck St. PO1	25 F3	Bramble La. SO31	4 C4
		Bedenham La. PO13	17 F5	Bramble Way. PO13	16 C6
		Bedford St. PO12	21 F4	Bramham Moor. PO15	15 F6
		Bedford St. PO5	25 H4	Bramley Gdns. PO12	23 F5
		Beech Gro. PO12	23 E3	Brasenose Clo. PO14	13 G2
		Beech Rd. PO15	7 G4	Braunston Clo. PO6	11 F3
		Beechcroft Clo. PO15	7 E4	Brecon Clo. PO14	7 G5
		Beechcroft Rd. PO12	23 F3	Bredenbury Cres. PO6	11 H2

Bredon Walk. PO14	7 G6
Brenchley Clo. PO16	9 G6
Brendon Rd. PO14	7 F6
Breton Clo. PO15	5 G2
Brewer Clo. SO31	5 F5
Brewers La. PO13	17 E6
Brewers St. PO1	25 H2
Briar Clo. PO12	22 C3
Briarwood Clo. PO16	8 B5
Bridge Ind Est. PO16	8 D3
Bridge Rd. SO31	4 A1
Bridge St. PO14	6 C6
Bridgefoot Dri. PO16	8 D4
Bridgemary Av. PO13	17 F5
Bridgemary Gro. PO13	17 E3
Bridgemary Rd. PO13	17 E3
Bridgemary Way. PO13	17 E3
Brights Av. PO6	11 E2
Brigantine Rd. SO31	12 D2
Brighton Av. PO12	21 F2
Britain St. PO1	25 F3
Britten Rd. PO13	19 F4
Brixworth Clo. PO6	11 F3
Broad St. PO1	25 E5
Broadcut. PO16	8 C3
Broadlaw Walk. PO14	7 G6
Broadsands Dri. PO12	22 C3
Broadsands Walk. PO12	22 C3
Brockhurst Ind Site. PO12	21 F1
Brockhurst Rd. PO12	21 E2
Brodwick Av. PO12	23 E3
Bromyard Cres. PO6	11 H3
Brook Av. SO31	4 B6
Brook Clo. SO31	4 C6
Brook Farm Av. PO15	7 H4
Brook La. SO31	12 B2
Brookers La. PO13	16 D5
Brookfield Gdns. SO31	4 D5
Brookmeadow. PO15	7 H4
Brookside. PO13	16 D3
Brookside Dri. SO31	4 C6
Broom Way. PO13	19 G4
Broomfield Cres. PO13	20 B3
Brougham La. PO12	21 F4
Brougham Rd. PO5	25 H4
Brougham St. PO12	21 F4
Browndown Rd. PO12	22 B3
Browning Av. PO6	10 D2
Brownwich La. PO14	14 A4
Bruce Clo. PO16	8 A3
Brune La. PO13	20 A1
Brunel Way. PO15	5 H4
Brunswick St. PO5	25 H4
Bryher Bridge. PO6	11 F5
Bryher Island. PO6	11 F5
*Bryony Clo,	
Bilberry Clo. SO31	12 D1
Bryson Rd. PO6	11 H4
Buchan Av. PO15	5 G1
Buckingham St. PO1	25 H2
Bucklers Rd. PO12	21 H2
Bucksey Rd. PO13	20 B2
Bude Clo. PO6	11 E3
Bulbarrow Walk. PO14	7 G5
Bullfinch Ct. PO13	19 G3
Burgundy Clo. SO31	13 E1
Buriton Clo. PO16	10 C2
Burmese Clo. PO15	5 G2
Burnaby Rd. PO1	25 G3
Burnett Rd. PO12	21 F4
Burney Rd. PO12	22 D3
Burnham Wood. PO16	8 A2
Burnhams Walk. PO12	24 C4
Burnside. PO13	16 D3
Burnt House La. PO14	15 H5
Bury Clo. PO12	23 F2
Bury Cres. PO12	23 F2
Bury Hall La. PO12	22 D3
Bury Rd. PO12	23 E2
Bush St, East. PO5	25 H5
Bush St, West. PO5	25 G5
Butcher St. PO1	25 F3
Butser Walk. PO14	7 G6
Buttercup Way. SO31	4 D6
Butterfly Dri. PO6	11 F2
Bye Rd. SO31	4 C1
Byron Clo. PO16	8 A3
Cadgwith Pl. PO6	11 F4
Cador Rd. PO16	10 A5
Calabrese Rd. PO1	5 F2
Caldecote Walk. PO5	25 H4
Calshot Way. PO13	20 B1

26

*Camber Pl, White Hart Rd. PO1	25 E5
Camargue Clo. PO15	5 F1
Cambrian Walk. PO14	16 B1
Cambridge Grn. PO14	13 G1
Cambridge Junction. PO1	25 F4
Cambridge Rd. PO12	21 E4
Cambridge Rd. PO13	19 G5
Cambridge Rd. PO1	25 G4
Camcross Clo. PO6	11 F3
Camden St. PO12	21 G4
Camelot Cres. PO16	10 A3
Cameron Clo. PO13	17 E5
Camp Rd. PO13	17 F5
Campion Clo. SO31	12 D1
Cams Hill. PO16	8 D4
Camsbay Clo. PO16	9 F5
Cannock Walk. PO14	7 G6
Cannons Barn Clo. PO16	10 B3
Canoe Clo. SO31	13 E2
Canterbury Clo. PO13	20 B6
Canterbury Rd. PO14	15 G4
Capstan Gdns. SO31	5 G6
*Captains Row, White Hart Rd. PO1	25 E5
Carberry Dri. PO16	10 B5
Carbis Clo. PO6	11 F4
Cardinal Way. SO31	5 F6
Carisbrook Av. PO14	18 C1
Carisbrooke Rd. PO13	20 B1
Carless Clo. PO13	20 D3
Carlton Clo. PO12	24 A4
Carlton Rd. PO16	10 C2
Carlton Way. PO12	24 B3
Carlyle Rd. PO12	23 F1
Carne Pl. PO6	11 F4
Caroline Gdns. PO15	7 E3
Caroline Pl. PO12	21 H4
Carron Walk. PO14	7 G6
Cartwright Dri. PO15	6 B4
Cascades App. PO1	25 H2
Cask St. PO1	25 H2
Casper John Clo. PO14	18 D1
Caspian Clo. PO15	5 F2
Castle Clo. PO5	25 H5
Castle Gro. PO12	10 C4
Castle Rd. PO5	25 G6
Castle St. PO16	10 C4
Castle St. PO14	6 C6
Castle Trading Est. PO16	10 D4
Castle View. PO12	21 H2
Castle View Rd. PO16	10 C5
Catamaran Clo. SO31	12 D2
Catisfield Rd. PO15	7 E4
Catsfield La. PO15	6 D5
Cavanna Clo. PO13	16 D5
Cawtes Pl. PO16	8 C4
Cecil Gro. PO5	25 G6
Cecil Pl. PO5	25 G6
Cedar Clo. PO12	21 F1
Cedar Way. PO14	7 G5
Celandine Av. SO31	12 D1
Central Rd. PO16	10 A4
Centre Way. SO31	5 E5
Chadderton Gdns. PO1	25 G5
Chaffinch. PO16	9 F5
Chaffinch Way. PO13	19 G3
Chale Clo. PO13	17 E6
Chalkpit Rd. PO6	11 F2
Chalky Walk. PO14	10 B4
Chamberlain Gro. PO14	8 A6
Chancel Clo. SO31	5 F5
Chandlers Way. SO31	5 F3
Chantrell Walk. PO15	7 F2
Chantry Rd. PO12	21 F3
Chapel Rd. SO31	4 D3
Chapel Sq. PO12	21 F3
Chapel St. PO12	21 H2
Chapel St. PO5	25 G5
Chapelside. PO6	6 C5
Charden Rd. PO13	20 D2
Charfield Clo. PO14	7 F5
Chark La. PO13	19 G3
Charlemount Dri. PO16	8 D4
Charles Dickens St. PO1	25 H3
Charlesbury Av. PO12	22 D2
Charlotte Mews. PO12	23 E4
Charlotte St. PO1	25 H2
Charnwood. PO13	17 F6
Chartwell Clo. PO14	13 G1
Chatfield Rd. PO14	16 D4
Chatham Dri. PO1	25 F5
Chatsworth Clo. PO15	7 E4
Chaucer Av. PO6	10 D2
Chaucer Clo. PO16	8 A4
Chedworth Cres. PO16	11 F2
Cheltenham Cres. PO13	19 G4
Cheltenham Rd. PO6	11 G3
Cheriton Rd. PO12	21 F6
Cherque La. PO13	19 H3
Cherry Clo. PO13	19 H5
Cherry Walk. SO31	12 B3
Cherrygarth Rd. PO15	7 E5
Cherrytree Av. PO14	7 F6
Chester Cres. PO13	20 B6
Chesterton Pl. PO15	5 G1
Chestnut Walk. PO12	21 G1
Chestnut Way. PO14	13 G2
Cheviot Grn. SO31	12 C3
Cheviot Walk. PO14	16 B1
Cheyne Way. PO13	19 H5
Chichester Clo. PO13	16 D6
Chichester Clo. SO31	4 C6
Chilcombe Clo. PO13	19 H5
Chilling La. SO31	12 D6
Chiltern Walk. PO14	7 H6
Chilworth Gro. PO12	21 G5
Chine Clo. SO31	5 E5
Church Clo. SO31	5 F5
Church La. SO31	4 A1
Church Path. PO16	8 C4
Church Path. PO14	24 C4
Church Path. PO14	6 C5
Church Pl. PO16	8 C4
Church Rd. PO12	23 E4
Church Rd. Locks Heath. SO31	5 F6
Church Rd, Warsash. SO31	12 B2
Church St. PO14	6 C5
Churcher Clo. PO12	22 C2
Churcher Walk. PO12	22 C2
Churchill Dri. PO14	13 G2
Cinderford Clo. PO6	11 G2
Circular Rd. PO1	25 G2
Civic Way. PO16	8 C4
Clan William Rd. PO13	19 G5
Clare Clo. PO14	13 G1
Clarence Rd. PO12	24 B3
Clarence St. PO1	25 H1
Clarendon Cres. PO14	13 G2
Clarendon Pl. PO1	25 H2
Claudia Ct. PO12	21 F4
Clayhall Rd. PO12	23 E4
Clee Av. PO14	7 F5
Cleeve Clo. PO6	11 G3
Cleric Ct. PO14	5 H6
Cleveland Dri. PO14	7 G5
Cleveland Rd. PO12	23 F2
Cliff Rd. PO14	18 B1
Clifton Rd. PO13	19 H6
Clifton St. PO12	21 F4
Clipper Clo. SO31	12 C2
Clive Gro. PO16	10 B5
Clock St. PO1	25 E3
Clover Clo. SO31	4 D6
Clover Clo. PO13	16 D5
Clyde Rd. PO12	21 F4
Clydesdale Rd. PO15	5 F2
Coach Hill. PO14	6 B6
Coal Park La. SO31	4 C1
Coastguard Clo. PO12	22 D4
Cobden St. PO12	21 G5
Cockerell Clo. SO31	5 G3
Cockleshell Clo. SO31	12 D1
Coghlan Clo. PO16	8 B4
Coldeast Clo. SO31	4 D4
Coldeast Way. SO31	5 E4
Colenso Rd. PO16	8 B4
Coleridge Clo. SO31	12 C2
Coleridge Rd. PO6	10 D2
Colesbourne Rd. PO6	11 F3
Colinton Av. PO16	10 C3
College La. PO1	25 F3
College Rd. PO1	25 E2
College St. PO1	25 F3
Collington Cres. PO6	11 G3
Colpoy St. PO5	25 G4
Coltsfoot Dri. SO31	4 D6
Coltsmead. PO6	11 E4
Commercial Rd. PO1	25 H3
Common Barn La. PO13	19 H5
Common Barn Rd. PO13	19 H3
Common La. PO14	6 A6
Compass Point. PO16	8 B5
Compton Clo. PO13	19 H5
Condor Av. PO13	9 F5
Conference Dri. SO31	5 F6
Conifer Gro. PO13	16 D4
Coniston Walk. PO14	7 G6
Connaught La. PO6	10 D3
Connemara Cres. PO15	5 F2
Connigar Clo. PO13	20 C3
Conqueror Way. PO14	19 E1
Constable Clo. PO12	23 G4
Coombe Farm Av. PO16	8 B5
Coombe Rd. PO12	21 G3
Coombedale. SO31	13 F1
Cooper Gro. PO16	10 C5
Copper St. PO5	25 G5
Coppice Way. PO15	7 F3
Coppins Gro. PO16	10 B5
Copse La. PO13	20 C1
Coracle Clo. SO31	12 D2
Coral Clo. PO16	10 B5
Corfe Clo. PO14	18 C1
Coriander Way. PO15	5 H1
Cormorant Clo. PO16	9 F5
Cormorant Walk. PO13	16 D6
Coronway La. PO16	10 A4
Cornfield. PO16	8 B2
Cornfield Rd. PO13	19 G4
Cornflower Clo. SO31	4 D6
Cornwell Clo. PO13	20 C3
Coronado Rd. PO12	21 G3
Cort Way. PO15	7 E2
Corvette Av. SO31	13 E2
Cotswold Walk. PO14	7 G6
Cottage Clo. PO12	23 F1
Cottage Gro. PO5	25 H5
Cottes Way. PO14	18 C1
Cottesway East. PO14	18 C1
Coulmere Rd. PO12	21 F4
Country Vw. PO14	15 F4
Coursepark Cres. PO14	13 H1
Court Barn Clo. PO13	19 G3
Court Barn La. PO13	19 G3
Court Rd. PO13	19 G4
Coverack Way. PO6	11 F5
Cow La. PO16	10 C5
Coward Rd. PO12	23 E4
Cowdray Pk. PO14	15 E6
Cowes La. SO31	12 C5
Cowslip Clo. PO13	16 D6
Cowslip Clo. SO31	12 D1
Coxdale. PO14	13 G2
Crableck La. SO31	4 B4
Crabthorne Farm La. PO14	15 F5
Cranbourne Rd. PO12	23 G2
Cranbourne Walk. PO14	16 A1
Cranleigh Rd. PO. PO16	9 G6
Craven Ct. PO15	7 G3
Crawford Dri. PO16	7 H2
Credenhill Rd. PO6	11 H3
Creek Rd. PO12	24 B4
Cremyll Clo. PO14	19 E1
Crescent Rd PO16	8 B5
Crescent Rd. PO12	23 E4
Crescent Rd. SO31	13 E1
Crest Clo. PO16	9 E4
Crispen Clo. SO31	5 F5
Croftlands Av. PO14	15 G5
Crofton Av. PO13	19 E3
Crofton La. PO14	18 C2
Crofton Way. PO31	12 A1
Cromerty Rd. PO14	15 F5
Cromhall Clo. PO14	7 F5
Crompton Way. SO31	5 G4
Crooked Walk La. PO17	10 D1
Cross Rd. PO13	19 H6
Cross St. PO1	25 F2
Crossfell Walk. PO14	7 G6
Crossland Clo. PO12	23 G3
Cuckoo La. PO14	15 F5
Culloden Clo. PO15	7 H3
Cumber Rd. SO31	4 D5
Cumberland St. PO1	25 F2
Cunningham Dri. PO12	17 F4
Cunningham Dri. SO31	5 F5
Curlew Dri. PO16	9 F5
Curlew Walk. PO13	16 C5
Curtiss Gdns. PO12	21 F5
Curzon Howe Rd. PO1	25 F3
Cutlers La. PO14	15 G5
Cutter Av. SO31	12 C1
Cygnet. PO16	9 F5
Cyprus Rd. PO14	13 G1
Daisy La. PO12	23 F2
Daisy La. SO31	5 G6
Dale Dri. PO13	16 D3
Dale Rd. PO14	15 H5
Dalewood Rd. PO15	7 F4
Dallington Clo. PO14	19 E2
Dampier Clo. PO13	20 C3
Dandelion Clo. PO13	16 D5
Danes Rd. PO16	10 A2
Darren Clo. PO14	15 H4
Davis Clo. PO13	20 C2
Dayshes Clo. PO13	16 D5
Deacon Rd. SO31	5 F6
Dean Clo. PO14	15 G4
Dean St. PO1	25 F3
Deane Gdns. PO13	19 H4
Deanes Park Rd. PO16	8 D5
Deansgate. PO14	19 E1
Deerhurst Cres. PO6	11 F2
Defiance Rd. PO1	25 F4
Delft Clo. SO31	4 D5
Dell Quay Clo. PO13	16 C6
Dellfield Clo. PO6	11 F3
Delme Dri. PO16	8 D4
Denbigh Dri. PO16	8 A3
Dene Clo. SO31	4 D5
Denham Clo. PO14	15 G6
Denville Av. PO16	10 C5
Derlyn Rd. PO16	8 B4
Derwent Clo. PO14	15 H4
Derwent Rd. PO13	19 G5
Desborough Clo. PO6	11 F3
Devonshire Way. PO14	7 E6
Dewar Clo. SO31	5 G4
Diamond St. PO5	25 G5
Diana Clo. PO12	22 D2
Dibles Rd. SO31	12 C2
Dieppe Gdns. PO12	23 E1
Dingle Way. SO31	5 F4
Discovery Clo. PO14	15 G3
Ditton Clo. PO14	15 G4
Dock Rd. PO12	23 G2
Dolman Rd. PO12	23 G3
Dolphin Cres. PO12	23 G3
Dolphin Ct. PO14	15 F4
Dolphin Way. PO1	23 G4
Dolphin Way. PO1	25 E4
*Dominie Walk, Smeeton Rd. PO13	19 G4
Donnelly St. PO12	21 F4
Dore Av. PO16	10 A3
Dormington Rd. PO6	11 G2
Dormy Clo. SO31	4 C5
Dormy Way. PO13	20 B1
Dorothy Dymond St. PO1	25 H3
Dorrien Rd. PO12	21 G3
Dorstone Rd. PO6	11 H2
Dove Gdns. SO31	5 F4
Dover Clo. PO14	15 F5
Downend Rd. PO16	9 F5
Downland Clo. SO31	5 E5
Downside. PO13	17 F6
Drake Clo. SO31	5 F4
Drake Rd. PO13	19 E3
Drift Rd. PO16	8 D3
Droxford Clo. PO12	21 F6,
Dryden Av. PO6	10 D3
Dryden Clo. PO16	8 A4
Dugald Drummond St. PO1	25 H3
Duisberg Way. PO5	25 G6
Dukes Rd. PO12	21 G4
Duncan Dri. PO14	6 D6
Duncan Rd. SO31	5 F3
Duncton Way. PO13	16 D5
Dundee Clo. PO15	7 G3
Dunkeld Rd. PO12	21 F3
Dunsmore Clo. PO5	25 H4
Dunstable Walk. PO14	7 F6
Durham St. PO12	21 F4
Durham St. PO1	25 H3
Durley Rd. PO12	21 F4
Dursley Cres. PO6	11 H4
Eagle Clo. PO16	9 F6
Earls Rd. PO16	8 B6
Earlsdon St. PO5	25 H4
East Cams Clo. PO16	9 F5
East Cliff Clo. PO13	19 G3
East Hill Clo. PO16	8 D4
East House Av. PO14	15 H6
East Lodge. PO15	7 E5
East St, Fareham. PO16	8 C5
East St, Portchester. PO16	10 C4
East St. PO5	25 E5
East St, Tichfield. PO16	6 C5
East Surrey St. PO1	25 H3
Eastbourne Av. PO12	21 F2
Eastbrook Clo. PO12	21 E2
Eastbrook Clo, Locks Heath. SO31	5 E3
Eastcroft Rd. PO12	21 F5
Eastern Parade. PO16	8 C6
Eastern Way. PO16	8 C5
Eastfield Av. PO14	16 B2
Eden Rise. PO16	8 B5
Eden St. PO1	25 H2
Edgar Cres. PO16	10 C5
Edgecombe Cres. PO13	20 B2
Edinburgh Rd. PO1	25 G2
Edney Path. SO31	4 C3
Edward Gro. PO16	10 D2
Elder Clo. SO31	12 D1
Eldon St. PO5	25 H4
Elgar Clo. PO12	23 E4
Elgar Clo. PO6	10 D4
Elgin Clo. PO15	7 H3
Elizabeth Ct. PO14	16 B1

Elizabeth Pl. PO12	21 H5
Elizabeth Rd. PO14	15 H6
Elkstone Rd. PO6	11 F2
Ellachie Gdns. PO12	23 F4
Ellachie Mews. PO12	23 F5
Ellachie Rd. PO12	23 F5
Ellerslie Clo. PO12	18 C2
Elm Gro. PO12	23 F1
Elm Gro. PO5	25 H5
Elm St. PO5	25 G5
Elmadale Clo. SO31	12 C2
Elmhurst Rd. PO16	8 B5
Elmhurst Rd. PO12	23 G2
Elmore Av. PO13	19 H6
Elmore Clo. PO13	19 H5
Elmore Rd. PO13	19 H6
Elms Rd. PO16	8 B6
Elphinstone Rd. PO5	25 H6
Elsfred Rd. PO14	18 C1
Elson La. PO12	21 F2
Elson Rd. PO12	21 F2
Embsay Rd. SO31	4 B1
Emmanuel Clo. PO14	13 G1
Endeavour Clo. PO12	24 B4
Endofield Clo. PO14	16 B2
Ennerdale Rd. PO14	15 H4
Enterprise Clo. SO31	12 C2
Epson Walk. PO13	19 H4
Eric Rd. PO14	15 G6
Erica Clo. SO31	5 E6
Esmonde Clo. PO13	19 G4
Esplanade. PO12	24 D4
Esplanade. PO13	19 F5
Ewer Common. PO12	23 F3
Exchange Rd. PO1	25 G3
Exeter Clo. SO31	5 E6
Exmoor Clo. PO15	5 G2
Exmouth Rd. PO12	21 F2
Exton Gdns. PO16	10 B2
Fairacre Rise. PO14	6 D6
Fairacre Walk. PO14	6 D6
Fairfield Av. PO14	7 G6
Fairholme Clo. PO12	21 G3
Fairisle Clo. PO14	15 F5
Fairthorne Gdns. PO12	21 G6
Fairview Ct. PO13	20 D6
Fairwater Rd. PO13	20 B1
Falcon Clo. PO6	9 F6
Falmouth Rd. PO6	11 E3
Fareham Heights. PO16	9 E3
Fareham Ind Park. PO16	8 D3
Fareham Park Rd. PO15	7 E2
Fareham Rd. PO13	21 E1
Farm Edge Rd. PO14	18 D1
Farm Rd. PO14	6 B4
Farmlea. PO6	11 E4
Faroes Clo. PO14	15 F5
Farrier Way. PO16	16 D2
Farriers Walk. PO12	23 H1
Farthing La. PO1	25 F5
Fastnet Wy. PO14	15 F5
Fay Clo. PO14	15 G6
Fayre Rd. PO16	8 B6
Felix Rd. PO12	21 G3
Fell Clo. SO31	5 F5
Fell Dri. PO13	19 G3
Fern Way. PO15	6 A3
Ferncroft Clo. PO14	19 E1
Ferndale Mews. PO13	16 D4
Ferneham Rd. PO15	7 F4
Fernie Clo. PO14	15 F6
Ferrol Rd. PO12	21 H4
Fey Rd. PO12	24 A3
Field Clo. SO31	13 F1
Field Clo. PO13	16 D3
Fieldhouse Dri. PO13	19 H3
Fieldmore Rd. PO12	21 G3
Filmer Clo. PO13	20 C2
Findon Rd. PO12	21 G2
Finnisterre Clo. PO14	15 F4
Fisguard Rd. PO12	21 G3
Fisher Clo. PO14	15 G5
Fisher Rd. PO13	17 E5
Fisher Rd. PO1	25 E4
Fishermans Walk. PO16	10 C4
Fishers Hill. PO15	6 D4
Fitzgerald Clo. PO15	5 G1
Fitzherbert St. PO1	25 H1
Fitzpatrick Ct. PO6	11 H3
Fitzwilliam Av. PO14	15 E6
Five Post La. PO14	21 G4
Flamingo Ct. PO16	9 F6
Flathouse Rd. PO1	25 H1
Fleet Clo. PO13	20 D1
Fleet End Bottom. SO31	12 D2
Fleet End Rd. SO31	12 D2
Fleming Clo. PO15	5 H4
Flint St. PO5	25 G5
Font Clo. PO	5 H6
Fontley La. PO15	6 C2
Ford Rd. PO12	21 F4
Forest Way. PO13	20 D1
Forneth Gdns. PO15	6 D5
Fort Fareham Ind Site. PO14	16 C2
Fort Fareham Rd. PO14	16 B2
Fort Rd. PO12	23 E4
Forth Clo. PO14	15 F5
Forties Clo. PO14	15 F4
Forton Rd. PO12	23 F1
Foster Clo. PO14	15 G4
Foster Rd. PO12	23 F2
Founders Way. PO13	17 F6
Fountain St. PO1	25 H2
Foxbury Gro. PO16	10 A5
Foxbury La. PO13	17 F4
Foxgloves. PO16	8 C2
Foxlea Gdns. PO12	21 G3
Foy Gdns. SO31	12 B2
Francis Clo. PO13	19 H5
Francis Pl. PO14	15 H6
Franklin Rd. PO13	20 B3
Fraser Rd. PO13	17 E4
Frater La. PO12	21 F2
Frederick St. PO1	25 H1
Freemantle Rd. PO12	21 G3
French St. PO1	25 F5
Friarspond La. PO15	7 E4
Frobisher Clo. PO13	20 C4
Frobisher Gro. PO16	10 B4
Frogmore. PO14	7 E6
Frosthole Clo. PO15	7 G2
Frosthole Cres. PO15	7 G3
Froxfield Gdns. PO16	10 B2
Fulmar Walk. PO13	16 C5
Funtley Hill. PO16	7 G1
Funtley Rd. PO16	7 G1
Furneaux Gdns. PO16	8 B2
Fury Way. PO14	15 F5
Furzehall Av. PO16	8 B2
Gainsborough Mews. PO14	6 C5
Gale Moor Av. PO12	22 C3
Galleon Clo. SO31	12 D1
Garden Courts. PO16	10 C4
Garden La. PO5	25 H6
Garden Mews. SO31	12 B2
Gardner Rd. PO14	6 C6
Garland Ct. PO12	21 G5
Garnett Clo. PO14	15 G4
Garstons Clo. PO14	6 B6
Garstons Rd. PO14	6 C6
Gatcombe Gdns. PO14	7 E5
Gatehouse Rd. PO16	10 A5
Gaylyn Way. PO14	7 E6
Geoffrey Cres. PO16	16 D1
George St. PO12	24 A3
Gibralter Clo. PO15	7 F4
Gibson Clo. PO13	19 H4
Gifford Clo. PO15	7 G3
Gilbert Clo. PO13	20 D2
Giles Clo. PO12	21 G4
Giles Clo. PO16	8 B2
Gilkicker Rd. PO12	23 G4
Gillcrest. PO14	5 G5
Girton Clo. PO14	13 G1
Gladstone Gdns. PO16	10 B5
Gladstone Rd. PO12	21 F3
Glebe Dri. PO13	20 C1
Glen Rd. SO31	4 D3
Glenbrook Walk. PO14	7 F6
Glenda Clo. PO31	12 B3
Glendale. SO31	13 F1
Glenelg. PO15	7 H3
Glenesha Gdns. PO15	7 F3
Glenthorne Clo. PO14	19 E2
Gloster Ct. SO31	5 G4
Gloucester Mews Vw. PO5	25 H5
Gloucester Pl. PO5	25 H5
Gloucester Rd. PO1	25 F2
Gloucester Ter. PO5	25 H5
Glyn Dri. PO14	15 G6
Glyn Way. PO14	15 G6
Godwit Clo. PO12	21 H2
Gold St. PO5	25 G5
Goldcrest Clo. PO16	9 E5
Goldfinch La. PO13	19 G3
Gomer La. PO12	22 C3
Goodsell Clo. PO14	15 F6
Goodwood. PO14	13 H1
Goodwood Clo. PO12	21 G2
Goodwood Rd. PO12	21 G6
Gordon Rd. PO12	21 G6
Gordon Rd. PO16	8 A4
Gordon Rd. PO1	25 G6
Gorran Av. PO12	20 C1
Gorse Clo. SO31	12 D1
Gorselands Way. PO13	20 C2
Gosport Rd. PO16	8 B6
Gosport Rd. PO13	19 H6
Gosport Rd. PO14	15 H5
Gould Clo. PO13	20 D4
Graham Rd. PO12	21 F4
Grand Parade. PO1	25 F5
Grange Clo. PO12	21 F4
Grange Cres. PO12	21 F4
Grange La. PO13	20 C3
Grange Rd. PO13	20 D6
Grasmere Way. PO14	15 H4
Grassymead. PO14	5 G5
Gray's Clo. SO31	13 E1
Grays Ct. PO1	25 F4
Grayshott Rd. PO12	21 F6
Great Gays. PO14	18 B1
Great Southsea St. PO5	25 G5
Grebe Clo. PO16	9 F6
Green Cres. PO13	20 C1
Green La,Alverstoke. PO12	23 E3
Green La, Fleet End. SO31	13 E2
Green La, Hardway. PO12	21 H3
Green La. SO31	4 B1
Green Link. PO13	19 G5
Green Rd. PO12	23 E4
Green Rd. PO5	25 H5
Green Rd. PO14	15 G4
Green Walk. PO15	7 G2
Green Wood Clo. PO16	8 B2
Greenaway La. SO31	12 B1
Greenbanks Gdns. PO16	8 D4
Greendale Clo. PO15	7 F2
Greenhollow Clo. PO16	7 H2
Greenlea Gro. PO12	21 E3
Greenway Rd. PO12	21 G4
Greetham St. PO1	25 H3
Gregson Av. PO13	17 E5
Gregson Clo. PO13	16 D5
Grenadier Clo. SO31	5 F6
Grenville Rd. PO13	19 F3
Greyfriars Rd. PO15	7 E4
Greyshott Av. PO14	7 E6
Grindle Clo. PO16	10 B2
Grosvenor St. PO5	25 H4
Grove Av. PO12	24 A3
Grove Av. PO16	10 B6
Grove Blds. PO12	23 G2
Grove Rd. PO12	21 G3
Grove Rd. PO16	8 A4
Grove Rd. PO13	19 F4
Grove Rd Sth. PO5	25 H6
Guardhouse Rd. PO1	25 G1
Gudge Heath La. PO15	7 F3
Guessens Path. PO14	6 C6
Guildhall Sq. PO1	25 H3
Guildhall Walk. PO5	25 H3
Guillemot Gdns. PO13	16 D5
Gull Clo. PO13	16 D6
Gun Wharf Rd. PO1	25 F5
Gunners Way. PO12	21 F2
Haddon Clo. PO14	7 G4
Half Moon St. PO1	25 E3
Halfpenny La. PO1	25 F5
Hallett Clo. PO14	15 G5
Halliday Clo. PO12	21 H5
Halsey Clo. PO12	23 E2
Ham La. PO12	21 G2
Hamble Clo. SO31	12 B2
Hamble Rd. PO12	21 F6
Hambrook Clo. PO12	21 F4
Hambrook St. PO5	25 G5
Hamilton Gro. PO13	16 D6
Hamilton Rd. PO16	10 D4
Hamlet Way. PO12	21 F1
Hammond Rd. PO15	7 G3
Hampshire Ter. PO5	25 G4
Hampton Gro. PO15	6 D5
Hanbidge Cres. PO15	17 E4
Hanbidge Walk. PO13	17 E4
Handley Rd. PO12	21 F4
Hanover Ct. PO1	25 F5
Hanover Gdns. PO16	8 B2
Hanover St. PO1	25 F3
Harbour Rd. PO12	24 C3
Harbour Tower. PO12	24 C4
Harbour Vw. PO16	10 B5
*Harbour Walk, Broad St. PO1	25 E5
Harcourt Rd. PO12	21 G5
Harcourt Rd. PO14	6 D6
Harding Rd. PO12	21 F4
Hardy Clo. SO31	5 F4
Harebell Clo. PO16	8 C2
Harlequin Gro. PO15	7 H4
Harold Rd. PO14	15 H5
Harrier Clo. PO13	19 H4
Harriet Clo. PO13	15 F6
Harris Rd. PO13	17 E4
Harrison Rd. PO16	8 B3
Harting Gdns. PO16	10 B?
Hartington Rd. PO12	21 F?
Hartlands Rd. PO16	8 B?
Harvester Dri. PO15	6 D?
Harvey Cres. SO31	13 E?
Harwood Clo. PO13	17 E?
Harwood Rd. PO14	17 E?
Haselworth Dri. PO12	23 F?
Haslar Bri. PO12	24 C?
Haslar Rd. PO12	24 B?
Haslar Sea Wall. PO12	23 H?
Hastings Av. PO12	21 F?
Hatherley Cres. PO16	9 H?
Hatherley Dri. PO16	9 H?
Hatherley Rd. PO6	11 F?
Havant St. PO1	25 E?
Havelock Rd. SO31	12 B?
Haven Cres. PO14	18 B?
Hawk Clo. PO14	15 F?
Hawke St. PO1	25 F?
Hawkins Rd. PO13	17 F?
Hawkwell. PO16	9 F?
Hawthorn Gdns. PO16	10 B?
Hawthorn La. SO31	4 C?
Hawthorn Walk. PO13	19 G?
Hayes Clo. PO15	7 F?
Hayling Clo. PO14	7 F?
Hazel Gro. SO31	5 G?
Hazelwood. PO14	15 F?
Headland Dri. SO31	5 E?
Heath La. PO14	14 C?
Heath Lawns. PO15	7 F?
Heath Rd. SO31	5 E?
Heath Rd North. SO31	4 D?
Heath Rd South. SO31	4 D?
Heather Clo. PO13	16 D?
Heather Gdns. PO15	7 F?
Heathfield Av. PO15	7 F?
Heaton Rd. PO12	21 F?
Hebrides Clo. PO14	15 F?
Hedley Clo. PO13	19 H?
Hedra Rd. SO31	5 E?
Helsby Clo. PO14	7 G?
Helsted Clo. PO12	22 C?
Helston Rd. PO6	11 E?
Hemingway Gdns. PO15	5 G?
Hempsted Rd. PO6	11 G?
Henley Gdns. PO15	7 G?
Henry St. PO12	24 B?
Henville Clo. PO13	20 D?
Herbert Rd. PO12	21 F?
Heron Way. PO13	16 D?
Herons Clo. PO14	15 G?
Hertsfield. PO14	5 G?
Heston Walk. PO12	22 C?
Hewett Clo. PO14	6 C?
Hewett Rd. PO14	6 C?
Hewitt Clo. PO12	21 F?
Hewitts Rise. SO31	12 B?
Hickley Path. PO16	8 D?
High Dri. PO13	20 B?
High Mead. PO15	7 G?
High Oaks Clo. SO31	5 E?
High St. SO31	4 A?
High St. PO16	8 C?
High St. PO12	24 C?
High St. PO13	19 G?
High St. PO1	25 F?
High St. PO14	6 C?
High Vw. PO16	10 B?
High Walk. PO15	7 G?
Highbury St. PO1	25 F?
Highcliff Rd. PO12	21 F?
Highfield Av. PO14	7 H?
Highfield Rd. PO12	21 F?
Highfields. SO31	12 D?
Highlands Rd. PO16	7 E?
Highnam Gdns. SO31	5 E?
Highwood Rd. PO13	20 C?
Hill Coppice Rd. PO15	5 H?
Hill Dri. PO15	7 G?
Hill Head Rd. PO14	18 B?
Hill Park Rd. PO12	21 E?
Hill Park Rd. PO15	7 F?
Hill Pl. PO31	4 A?
Hill Rd. PO16	10 B?
Hill View Rd. PO16	10 B?
Hill Walk. PO15	7 F?
Hillary Clo. PO16	7 H?
Hillbrow Clo. PO15	7 G?
Hillcroft. PO15	6 A?
Hiller Walk. PO13	19 H?
Hillside Cres. PO6	10 D?
Hillsley Rd. PO6	11 E?
Hillson Dri. PO15	7 E?
Hilton Rd. PO12	23 G?
Hispano Av. PO15	5 G?
Hobbs Passage. PO12	24 C?
Hoeford Clo. PO16	16 D?

Holbrook Rd. PO16 8 B5
Hollam Clo. PO14 6 D5
Hollam Cres. PO14 6 D5
Hollam Dri. PO14 6 D5
Holland Pk. SO31 4 D5
Holland Pl. PO13 17 E6
Holly Clo. SO31 4 C5
Holly Gro. PO16 7 G2
Holly Hill La. SO31 4 B5
Holly St. PO12 24 A4
Hollybank. PO13 19 G5
Hollybrook Gdns. SO31 5 F4
Hollywell Dri. PO6 11 F5
Holmdale Rd. PO12 21 F3
Holmefield Av. PO14 16 B2
Holmgrove. PO14 5 G6
Home Rule Rd. PO31 5 F5
Homer Clo. PO13 20 B2
Honey La. PO15 7 F1
Honeysuckle Clo. SO31 5 F4
Honeysuckle Clo. PO13 16 D5
Hood Clo. SO31 5 F5
Hook La. PO14 13 E3
Hook Park Rd. SO31 12 B4
Hope St. PO1 25 H2
Hopkins Clo. PO6 10 D4
Hornby Clo. SO31 12 C3
Hornet Clo. PO15 7 F3
Hornet Clo. PO12 23 G3
Horseshoe Clo. PO14 6 A4
Horseshoe Lodge. SO31 12 D1
Horton Rd. PO13 17 E4
Hospital La. PO16 10 D6
House Farm Rd. PO12 21 E6
Howe Rd. PO13 20 C5
Howerts Clo. SO31 12 C3
Hoylake Clo. PO12 20 C1
Hoylecroft Clo. PO15 7 G2
Humber Clo. PO14 15 F5
Hunter Clo. PO13 20 D3
Hunters Lodge. PO15 7 E5
Huntingdon Clo. PO14 13 G2
Huntley Clo. PO6 11 G3
Hunts Pond Rd. PO14 13 G1
Hurst Clo. PO14 18 C1
Hurst Grn. PO13 16 D6
Huxley Clo. SO31 13 G1
Hyde St. PO5 25 H5

Ilex Cres. SO31 5 E6
INDUSTRIAL ESTATES:
Apple Ind Est. SO31 5 G4
Barratt Ind Est. SO31 5 G4
Bridge Ind Est. PO16 8 D3
Brockhurst Ind Site. PO12 21 F1
Castle Trading Est. PO16 10 D4
Fareham Ind Park. PO16 8 D3
Fort Fareham Ind Site. PO14 16 C2
Newgate Lane Ind Est. PO14 16 C2
Segensworth East Ind Est. SO31 5 H4
Segensworth West Ind Est. SO31 5 G4
Solent 2 Business Park. PO15 5 G2
Speedfields Park. PO13 16 C3
Ingledene Clo. PO12 23 F2
Ingleside Clo. PO14 6 D6
Inverkip Clo. PO13 19 F3
Inverness Av. PO15 7 G3
Inverness Rd. PO12 21 G4
Ironbridge Cres. SO31 5 E3
Iron Mill Clo. PO15 7 F2
Iron Mill La. PO15 6 D1
Irvine Clo. PO14 8 A2
Isambard Brunel Rd. PO1 25 H3
Island View Walk. PO16 10 B2
Ivy La. PO1 25 F1

Jacobs St. PO1 25 H2
Jacomb Pl. PO13 17 F6
Jago Rd. PO1 25 E2
Jamaica Pl. PO12 23 G2
James Clo. PO13 17 E4
James Rd. PO14 16 D4
Jarvis Fields. SO31 4 A1
Jasmine Walk. PO14 7 G5
Jason Way. PO12 21 E2
Jay Clo. PO14 15 G3
Jellicoe Av. PO12 22 D4
Jerram Clo. PO12 22 D3
Jersey Clo. PO14 19 E2
Jervis Dri. PO12 21 G4
Jesmond Gro. SO31 13 F1
Jessie Rd. PO12 21 F6
Johns Rd. PO16 8 B6
Jonathan Rd. PO16 7 G4
Joseph St. PO12 24 A4

Jubilee Av. PO6 10 D3
Jubilee Ct. PO14 16 C1
Jubilee Rd. PO12 21 G5
Jubilee Rd. PO16 10 C4
Jubilee Ter. PO5 25 G5
Julie Av. PO15 7 G4
Jumar Clo. SO31 12 B3
Justin Clo. PO14 7 G5
Jute Clo. PO16 10 B3
Jutland Clo. PO15 5 G1

Kealy Rd. PO12 21 G4
Keast Walk. PO13 17 E4
Keats Av. PO6 10 D2
Keilder Gro. PO13 17 F6
Keith Clo. PO12 21 G4
Kelsey Clo. PO14 13 F1
Kelsey Head. PO6 11 F4
Kelvin Gro. PO16 10 C3
Kenilworth Clo. PO13 19 G4
Kennedy Av. PO15 7 G2
Kennedy Cres. PO12 22 D4
Kennet Clo. PO12 23 F4
Kensington Gdns. SO14 13 G1
Kensington Rd. PO12 23 G2
Kent Gro. PO16 10 B5
Kent Rd. PO5 25 G6
Kent Rd. PO13 16 D4
Kent St. PO1 25 F3
Kenwood Rd. PO16 10 C6
Kenya Rd. PO16 10 A4
Kestrel Clo. PO14 15 G4
Keyes Clo. PO13 17 E4
Keyes Rd. PO13 17 E5
Keyhaven Clo. PO13 16 C6
Kilmiston Dri. PO16 10 B2
Kiln Acre. PO16 8 B3
Kiln Rd. PO16 7 H2
Kilwich Way. PO16 10 A5
Kimpton Clo. PO13 19 H4
King Charles St. PO1 25 F5
*King Edward Ct, White Hart Rd. PO1 25 E5
King George Rd. PO16 10 B4
King Henry I St. PO1 25 G3
King John Av. PO16 10 A4
King Richard I Rd. PO1 25 G3
King St. PO12 24 B3
King St. PO5 25 H5
King William St. PO1 25 F2
Kingcup Av. SO31 4 D6
Kingdom Clo. PO15 5 H4
Kingfisher Copse. SO31 5 F6
Kingfishers. PO16 9 F6
Kings Rd. PO16 8 B5
Kings Rd. PO13 23 F1
Kings Rd. PO1 19 F4
Kings Rd. PO1 25 E2
Kings Rd. PO5 25 G5
Kings Ter. PO5 25 G5
Kingsbench Alley. PO1 25 F3
Kingscote Rd. PO6 11 E2
Kingsland Clo. PO6 11 H3
Kingsley Rd. PO12 21 F3
Kingsmead Av. PO14 19 E2
Kingsmill Clo. PO12 23 E2
Kingston Gdns. PO15 7 F1
Kingston Rd. PO12 21 F5
*Kingswell Path, Commercial Rd. PO1 25 H3
Kingswell St. PO1 25 H2
Kitescroft Clo. PO14 13 H2
Kittewake Clo. PO13 16 D6
Kneller Ct. PO16 7 H2
Knights Bank Rd. PO14 18 B1
Knights Clo. SO31 12 D2
Knotgrass Rd. SO31 12 D1
Kyak Clo. SO31 12 D2
Kynon Clo. PO12 21 H2

Laburnum Rd. PO16 16 D1
Ladram Rd. PO12 22 D2
Lakeside. PO16 7 G1
Lakeside. PO13 19 G6
Lambourn Clo. PO14 7 F5
Lambourne Dri. SO31 5 F6
Lancaster Clo. PO13 20 A6
Lancaster Clo. PO16 10 A2
Landon Ct. PO12 23 E4
Landon Rd. PO13 20 D2
Landport St. PO5 25 G4
Landport Ter. PO5 25 G4
Landport Vw. PO1 25 H2
Lands End Rd. SO31 4 A1
Lanes End. PO14 15 G6
Langstone Walk. PO14 7 F6
Langstone Walk. PO13 16 D6
Lansdown Av. PO16 10 C6
Lansdowne St. PO5 25 G4

Lanyard Dri. PO13 20 C4
Lapthorn Clo. PO13 16 D4
Lapwing Clo. PO12 21 H3
Lapwing Gro. PO16 9 F4
Larch Clo. PO13 19 H5
Larchdale Clo. SO31 12 C3
Larches Gdns. PO15 7 E5
Larkspur Clo. SO31 12 D1
Laser Clo. SO31 12 D1
Lasham Walk. PO14 7 F6
Laurel Clo. SO31 5 F5
Laurel Gdns. SO31 5 F5
Laurel Rd. SO31 5 F5
Laurus Walk. PO13 19 H4
Laverock Lea. PO16 10 B3
Lavinia Rd. PO12 23 F1
Lawn Clo. PO13 20 D2
Lawn Dri. SO31 13 F1
Lawrence Rd. PO15 7 H4
Lawson Clo. SO31 4 C1
Laxton Clo. SO31 5 F6
Layton Rd. PO13 17 E5
Lea Oak Gdns. PO15 7 F6
Leabrook. SO31 5 E4
Leamington Cres. PO13 19 G4
Lear Rd. PO12 23 F1
Lechlade Gdns. PO15 7 G1
Leckford Clo. PO16 10 B2
Ledbury Rd. PO6 11 G3
Lederle La. PO13 17 E3
Lee Rd. PO12 21 G4
Leep La. PO12 23 F4
Lees La. PO12 21 G5
Leesland Rd. PO12 21 F5
Leigh Rd. PO16 8 A4
Leith Av. PO16 10 C3
Lennox Clo. PO12 23 G5
Lennox Row. PO1 25 F2
Leominster Rd. PO6 11 F2
Leonard Rd. PO12 23 G1
Leopard St. PO1 25 F3
Lerryn Rd. PO13 17 F6
Lester Rd. PO12 21 E5
Leventhorpe Ct. PO12 23 G2
Leviathan Clo. PO14 15 H6
Levison Clo. PO12 22 D3
Leyland Clo. PO12 23 F3
Lichfield Rd. PO14 5 G6
Lime Gro. PO6 11 F2
Lincoln Clo. PO14 5 G6
Lind Clo. PO12 23 G5
Lind Way. SO31 5 E3
Linden Ct. SO31 5 G5
Linden Gro. PO12 23 F2
Linden Lea. PO16 10 B3
Link Way. PO14 19 E2
Linnet Clo. PO12 21 E4
Lion St. PO1 25 F3
Lion Ter. PO1 25 G3
Lipazzaner Fields. PO15 5 F1
Little Abshot Rd. SO31 5 G4
Little Anglesey Rd. PO12 23 E4
Little Britain St. PO1 25 F3
Little Chilworth. PO12 21 G5
Little Clo. PO13 17 E4
Little Gays. PO14 18 B1
Little Green. PO12 23 E3
Little Green Orchard. PO12 23 E3
Little La. PO13 23 E4
Little Park Farm Rd. SO31 5 G4
Little Southsea St. PO1 25 G5
Littlewood Gdns. SO31 4 D6
Lock App. PO6 11 E5
Lock View. PO6 11 F4
Locks Heath Park Rd. SO31 13 F1
Locks Rd. SO31 5 F6
Lockswood Rd. SO31 4 D6
Lodge Gdns. PO12 23 E2
Lodge Rd. SO31 5 F6
Lombard St. PO1 25 F5
Lombardy Clo. PO13 17 F6
Long Curtain Rd. PO1 25 F6
Long Drive. PO13 20 B1
Longacres. PO14 5 G5
Longdean Clo. PO6 11 E2
Longfield Av. PO13 7 F6
Longmynd Dri. PO14 7 F6
Longs La. PO14 15 G5
Longstaffe Gdns. PO13 7 H2
Longwater Dri. PO12 23 G5
Lonsdale Av. PO16 10 C6
Lord Montgomery Way. PO1 25 G4
Lovett Gro. PO15 7 F3
Lower Bellfield. PO14 6 B6
Lower Church Path. PO15 25 H3
Lower Church Rd. PO14 15 H4
Lower Duncan Rd. SO31 5 F3
Lower Quay. PO16 8 C6
Lower Quay Clo. PO16 8 B6

Lower Quay Rd. PO16 8 C6
Lower Spinney. SO31 12 B3
Lower Swanwick Rd. SO31 4 C1
Ludlow Rd. PO6 11 G3
Lulworth Rd. PO13 19 G5
Lundy Walk. PO14 15 F5
Lychgate Grn. PO14 15 G3
Lydney Clo. PO6 11 H3
Lydney Rd. SO31 5 E6
Lyndale Rd. SO31 5 G4
Lynden Clo. PO14 7 E6
Lyndhurst Rd. PO12 21 F6
Lynton Gdns. PO16 7 H2
Lysses Ct. PO16 8 C4
Lysses Path. PO16 8 C4
Mabey Clo. PO12 23 G4
Macaulay Av. PO6 11 E2
Madden Clo. PO6 22 D3
Maddison Ct. PO16 8 C5
Madison Clo. PO13 20 D2
Magdalene Way. PO14 13 G1
Magennis Clo. PO13 20 D3
Magnolia Clo. PO14 7 G6
Magpie La. PO13 19 G3
Main Rd. PO1 25 E2
Main Rd. PO1 25 E4
Maizemore Walk. PO13 19 G4
Malcolm Clo. SO31 5 G5
Malin Clo. PO14 15 F5
Mallard Gdns. PO13 16 D6
Mallory Cres. PO16 8 A3
Mallow Clo. SO31 4 D6
Malt House La. PO16 8 B4
Malus Clo. PO14 16 B1
Malvern Av. PO14 7 G6
Malvern Rd. PO12 21 F5
Mancroft Av. PO14 15 G6
Manor Ct. PO15 5 H4
Manor Way. PO13 19 G5
Mansfield Rd. PO13 20 B2
Mantle Clo. PO13 20 C3
Maple Clo. PO15 7 E5
Maple Clo. PO13 19 H5
Margarita Rd. PO15 7 G4
Margarys Ct. PO1 25 F3
Margold Clo. PO15 7 G4
Marina Keep. PO6 11 F5
Marina Gro. PO16 10 B5
Marine Parade East. PO13 19 F5
Marine Parade West. PO13 19 E3
Mariners Way. PO12 23 H3
Mariners Way. SO31 12 A2
Marken Clo. SO31 4 D5
Market Way. PO1 25 H2
Marks Rd. PO14 16 A6
Marks Tey Rd. PO14 15 G3
Marlborough Gro. PO16 10 B5
Marlborough Rd. PO12 21 E4
Marlborough Row. PO1 25 F2
Marles Clo. PO13 20 D2
Marlin Clo. PO13 20 C4
Marlow Clo. PO15 7 G1
Marsden Rd. PO6 11 G3
Marsh La. PO14 15 E6
Martello Clo. PO13 22 C3
Martells Ct. PO1 25 F4
Martha St. PO1 25 H1
Martin Av. PO14 15 H6
Martin Clo. PO13 19 G3
Mary Rose Clo. PO15 7 G2
Masefield Av. PO6 10 D2
Masten Cres. PO13 20 C2
Mayfield Clo. PO14 15 H5
Mayfield Rd. PO12 23 G3
Mayflower Clo. PO14 19 E1
Maylings Farm Rd. PO16 7 H3
Maynard Clo. PO13 17 E4
Mayridge. PO14 5 G5
Mays La. PO14 15 G5
Maytree Clo. SO31 5 E6
Maytree Gdns. PO. PO16 8 A5
Maytree Rd. PO16 8 A5
Mead Way. PO16 8 B3
Meadcroft Clo. SO31 12 B3
Meadow Av. SO31 5 F5
Meadow St. PO5 25 G5
Meadow Walk. PO15 16 D3
Meadowbank Rd. PO15 7 F4
Meadowsweet Way. PO6 11 F2
Melbourne St. PO5 25 H4
Melrose Gdns. PO12 21 E3
Mendips Rd. PO14 7 G6
Mendips Walk. PO14 7 F6
Meon Clo. PO13 16 D6
Meon Rd. PO14 14 C4
Merganser Clo. PO12 21 H3
Meriden Rd. PO5 25 G4

Merlin Gdns. PO16	10 B2	Newbroke Rd. PO13	20 D2	Osborne Rd. PO13	19 F4	Pipit Clo. PO12	21 H3
Merrow Clo. PO16	9 G5	Newgate La. PO14	16 C5	Osborne Rd. SO31	12 B3	Pitchponds Rd. SO31	12 B3
Merryfield. PO14	5 G5	Newgate Lane Ind Est. PO14	16 C2	Osborne View Rd. PO14	18 C1	Place House Clo. PO15	7 F4
Merstone Rd. PO13	17 E6	Newgate Rd. PO14	16 C5	Oslands La. SO31	4 B2	Plover Clo. PO14	15 F5
Merton Av. PO16	10 C6	Newlands. PO15	7 E4	Osprey Clo. PO13	19 H4	Plymouth Dri. PO14	15 E6
Merton Cres. PO16	10 C5	Newlands Av. PO12	21 F6	Osprey Ct. PO16	9 F5	Pond Rd. SO31	4 D3
Middle Mead. PO14	6 D6	Newlyn Way. PO6	11 F4	Oval Gdns. PO12	22 D2	Pook La. PO17	8 B1
Middle St. SO31	5 F4	Newport Rd. PO12	21 E5	Owen Clo. PO13	20 C3	Poplar Dri. PO14	7 G6
Middle St. PO5	25 H4	Newton Clo. PO14	15 G3	Oxford Clo. PO16	8 A3	Port Solent. PO6	11 E5
Middlecroft La. PO12	21 F4	Newton Pl. PO13	19 F4	Oxford Rd. PO12	21 E5	Port Way. PO6	11 G5
Middleton Clo. PO14	7 G6	Newtown. PO16	10 C3	Oxleys Clo. PO14	6 D6	Portal Rd. PO13	17 E5
Middleton Walk. PO14	7 G6	Newtown Rd. SO31	12 B3	Oyster Mews. PO1	25 F5	Portchester La. PO17	10 C4
Midfield Clo. PO14	16 B1	Nicholas Cres. PO15	7 H4	Oyster Quay. PO6	11 G5	Portchester Rd. PO16	8 D5
Midways. PO14	18 D1	Nicholl Pl. PO13	17 E6	Oyster St. PO1	25 F5	Portland Dri. PO12	22 C3
Mile End Rd. PO1	25 H1	Nickel St. PO5	25 G5			Portland Rd. PO5	25 H6
Military Rd. PO1	25 G1	Nightingale Clo. PO12	21 E4	Paddock Walk. PO6	11 E4	Portland St. PO16	8 C5
Military Rd. PO12	20 D6	Nightingale Mews. SO31	5 F6	Paffard Clo. PO13	20 C3	Portland St. PO1	25 F3
Military Rd. PO16	8 D3	Nightingale Rd. PO5	25 G6	Paget Rd. PO12	23 E4	Portobello Gro. PO16	9 E4
Mill La. PO12	21 H4	Nimrod Dri. PO13	20 C4	Painswick Clo. PO6	11 G3	Portsdown Hill Rd. PO17	10 A1
Mill La. PO1	25 H1	Nine Elms La. PO17	8 D1	Painswick Clo. SO31	4 D3	Portsdown Rd. PO16	10 A4
Mill La. PO15	6 C3	Niton Clo. PO13	17 E6	Pallant Gdns. PO16	8 D4	Portsmouth Rd. PO13	20 A6
Mill Pond Rd. PO12	21 G4	Nobbs La. PO1	25 F4	Palmerston Av. PO16	8 C4	Portview Av. PO6	10 C3
Mill Rd. PO12	21 F4	Nobes Av. PO13	17 E5	Palmerston Dri. PO14	16 C1	Portview Gdns. PO16	10 C3
Mill Rd. PO16	8 B6	Nobes Clo. PO13	17 F6	Palmerston Rd. PO6	25 H6	Posbrook La. PO14	14 C3
Mill St. PO14	6 C5	Norfolk Rd. PO12	21 E3	Palmerston Way. PO12	22 D4	Postern Clo. PO16	10 C4
Miller Dri. PO16	7 H2	Norfolk St. PO5	25 H5	Palmyra Rd. PO12	21 G3	Potters Av. PO16	8 A2
Milton Gro. SO31	13 G1	Norgett Way. PO16	10 B5	Palomino Dri. PO15	5 F2	Pound Clo. PO13	20 D2
Milvill Rd. PO13	19 F4	Norman Clo. PO16	10 C5	Pamela Av. PO6	11 E3	Poundgate Dri. PO14	13 G2
Minster Clo. PO15	7 E4	Norman Rd. PO12	21 F5	Pan St. PO1	25 H2	Poyner Clo. PO15	8 B4
Mirror Clo. SO31	13 E1	Normandy Clo. PO12	23 E1	Pannall Rd. PO12	21 F3	Poynings Pl. PO1	25 F5
Mistletoe Gdns. SO31	4 C3	Norset Rd. PO15	7 F3	Paradise La. PO16	9 E4	Prelate Way. PO14	13 H1
Mitchell Clo. PO15	5 H4	North Clo. PO12	22 D2	Paradise St. PO1	25 H2	Prideaux-Brune Av. PO13	17 E4
Moat Dri. PO12	22 C2	North Cross St. PO12	24 C4	Parham Rd. PO12	21 H4	Primate Rd. PO14	13 H1
Moat Walk. PO12	22 C2	North Hill. PO16	8 B2	Park Clo. PO12	21 E4	Primrose Clo. PO13	17 E3
Molesworth Rd. PO12	23 G2	North Path. PO13	20 C4	Park Farm Av. PO15	7 F2	Primrose Way. SO31	12 D1
Monarch Clo. SO31	13 F1	North St. PO12	24 B4	Park La. PO16	8 B4	Prince Alfred St. PO12	23 F2
Monckton Rd. PO12	23 F5	North St. PO12	21 F4	Park La. PO14	15 G5	Prince George St. PO1	25 F2
Monks Hill. PO14	19 E3	North St. PO1	25 F2	Park Rd. PO12	23 F3	Prince of Wales Rd. PO2	24 B4
Monks Way. PO14	18 C2	North Wallington. PO16	8 C3	Park Rd. PO1	25 F4	Prinsted Walk. PO14	7 F6
Monroe Clo. PO12	22 C2	Northarbour Rd. PO6	11 H4	Park St. PO13	23 F1	Priory Rd. PO12	21 G2
Monterey Dri. SO31	13 E1	Northarbour Spur. PO6	11 H4	Park St. PO12	24 A4	Priory Rd. PO15	7 E3
Montgomery Rd. PO13	17 E4	Northcott Clo. PO12	22 E3	Park St. PO5	25 G4	Privett Pl. PO12	21 E6
Montpelier Clo. SO31	5 G6	Northcroft Rd. PO12	21 F4	Park Walk. PO15	7 F3	Privett Rd. PO15	7 E3
Montrose Av. PO16	10 D2	Northfield Av. PO14	16 B1	Parker Clo. PO12	21 F1	Privett Rd. PO12	22 A2
Montserrat Rd. PO13	19 F4	Northfield Park. PO16	9 H4	Parkglen. SO31	5 G5	Puffin Cres. PO14	15 F4
Monument La. PO17	9 H1	Northmore Clo. SO31	5 F4	Parklands. SO31	5 E5	Puffin Gdns. PO13	16 D5
Moody Rd. PO14	18 D1	Northmore Rd. SO31	5 F4	Parklands Clo. PO12	21 G4	Pump La. PO13	20 C1
Moore Gdns. PO12	21 F6	Northway. PO13	17 E4	Parklands Ct. PO12	21 E6	Purbeck Dri. PO14	7 F6
Moorland Clo. SO31	5 E5	Northways. PO14	15 H6	Parr Rd. PO6	11 H4	Purbeck St. PO1	25 F3
Moraunt Clo. PO12	21 H2	Northwood Sq. PO16	8 B4	Parry Clo. PO6	10 D3	Purbeck Walk. PO14	7 F6
Moraunt Dri. PO16	10 A5	Norton Clo. PO16	8 A3	Partridge Clo. PO16	9 E5	Pye St. PO1	25 H2
Moreland Rd. PO12	23 F1	Norwich Clo. SO31	4 C5	Passage La. SO31	12 A2	Pyrford Clo. PO12	21 G2
Morgans Dri. PO14	15 G3	Norwich Pl. PO13	19 F3	Patchway Dri. PO14	7 F5	Pytchley Clo. PO14	15 E6
Morningside Av. PO16	10 D3	Nottingham Pl. PO13	19 F4	Paxton Rd. PO13	8 A5	
Morris Clo. PO13	16 D3	Nursery Clo. PO13	16 D5	Peacock Clo. PO16	9 E6	Quay Haven. SO31	4 B1
Morshead Cres. PO16	8 A3	Nursery La. PO14	19 E1	Peacock La. PO1	25 F5	Quay La. PO12	21 G1
Mortimer Rd. PO6	11 G3	Nutash. PO14	5 G5	Peak Dri. PO14	7 F5	Quay St. PO16	8 C5
Mortimore Rd. PO12	21 F4	Nyewood Av. PO16	10 C2	Peak La. PO14	7 F6	Queen Mary Rd. PO16	9 G6
Mound Clo. PO12	23 E2	Nyria Way. PO12	23 H2	Pearce Ct. PO12	24 A3	Queen St. PO1	25 E3
Mount Dri. PO15	6 D5			Peartree Clo. PO14	15 H5	Queens Clo. PO13	19 F4
Mount Pleasant Rd. PO12	23 F3	Oak Rd. PO15	7 F4	Peel Rd. PO12	24 A3	Queens Cres. PO5	25 H6
Mountbatten Clo. PO13	17 E4	Oak St. PO12	24 A4	Pelham Rd. PO12	21 G5	Queens Cres. PO14	15 H5
Mountview Av. PO16	10 D3	Oakcroft La. PO14	15 G3	Pelham Rd. PO5	25 H5	Queens Gro. PO5	25 H6
Mousehole Rd. PO6	11 E3	Oakdene. PO13	20 D1	Pelican Clo. PO15	7 F3	Queens Pl. PO5	25 H6
Mulberry Av. PO14	19 E2	Oakdown Rd. PO14	15 H5	Pembroke Clo. PO1	25 F5	Queens Rd. PO16	8 B5
Mulberry Clo. PO12	23 F2	Oaklands Gdns. PO14	13 G2	Pembroke Cres. PO14	18 C1	Queens Rd. PO12	23 G1
Mullion Clo. PO6	11 G5	Oaklands Way. PO14	13 G2	Pembroke Clo. PO1	25 F5	Queens Rd. PO13	19 G6
Mumby Rd. PO12	24 B3	Oakwood Clo. SO31	12 C3	Pembury Rd. PO14	15 H3	Queens Rd. PO12	25 E2
Murray Clo. PO15	7 G3	Occupation La. PO14	6 A6	Pendennis Rd. PO6	11 E3	Queens Rd. SO31	12 B2
Murrays La. PO1	25 E2	Ocean Clo. PO15	7 F3	Penhale Gdns. PO14	13 F2	Queens Way. PO5	25 H6
Museum Rd. PO1	25 G5	Ockenden Clo. PO5	25 H5	Penn Way. PO12	22 D2	Quintrell Av. PO16	9 G6
Mustang Av. PO15	5 F2	Odell Clo. PO16	7 H2	Pennine Walk. PO14	7 G6	
Myrtle Av. PO16	10 C4	Olave Clo. PO15	19 G4	Pennine Way. PO13	20 A6	Racecourse La. PO6	11 G4
Myrtle Clo. PO16	16 D5	Old Commercial Rd. PO1	25 H1	Pennington Way. PO15	7 F2	Radclyffe Rd. PO16	8 D3
		Old Common. SO31	5 F5	Penny St. PO1	25 F5	Radnor St. PO5	25 H4
Nailsworth Rd. PO6	11 G3	Old Common Gdns. SO31	5 E5	Pennycress. SO31	12 D1	Raglan Ct. PO5	5 F4
Naish Dri. PO12	21 G1	Old Farm La. PO14	18 D1	Pentland Rise. PO16	10 C2	Raley Rd. SO31	13 E1
Napier Cres. PO15	7 E4	Old Garden Clo. SO31	5 G6	Pepys Clo. PO12	23 F5	Rampart Row. PO12	24 C5
Naseby Clo. PO6	11 F2	Old Gosport Rd. PO16	8 B6	Percy Rd. PO12	23 G2	Ramsay Pl. PO13	17 E6
Nashe Clo. PO15	7 F3	Old Rd. PO12	23 G3	Pershore Clo. SO31	5 F6	Rannoch Clo. PO15	7 G3
Nashe Way. PO15	7 E3	Old St. PO14	15 E6	Persian Dri. PO15	5 F2	Ransome Clo. PO14	6 B6
Nasmith Clo. PO12	22 C2	Old Swanwick La. SO31	4 B1	Perth Rd. PO13	17 E5	Ranvilles La. PO14	6 D6
Navy Rd. PO1	25 F1	Old Turnpike. PO16	8 B2	Peters Clo. SO31	4 D6	Rapson Clo. PO6	11 H3
Neelands Gro. PO6	10 D4	Oldbury Way. PO14	7 F5	Peters Rd. SO31	4 D6	Ravens Clo. PO14	15 H5
Nelson Av. PO16	10 A4	Oldenburg. PO15	5 F1	Petrel Walk. PO13	16 D6	Ravenswood. PO14	5 G6
Nelson Ct. PO14	16 B2	Oldstar Pl. PO1	25 E3	Petrie Rd. PO13	19 G4	Raymond Rd. PO6	10 D3
Nelson La. PO17	10 B1	Oleander Clo. SO31	5 F4	Pettycot Cres. PO13	16 D5	Raynes Rd. PO13	19 H6
Nelson Rd. PO12	23 F2	Olive Cres. PO16	10 C5	Phoenix Way. PO13	20 C1	Rectory Clo. PO12	23 E4
Nepean Clo. PO12	23 F5	Orange Gro. PO13	20 D1	Pier Rd. PO5	25 G6	Rectory Clo. PO14	15 G5
Neptune Rd. PO15	7 F3	Orchard Clo. PO12	21 F1	Pier St. PO13	19 F5	Red Barn La. PO15	7 G1
Nesbitt Clo. PO15	16 D5	Orchard Gro. PO16	10 A5	Pilgrims Way. PO14	18 D2	Redbarn Av. PO16	10 B3
Netherton Rd. PO12	21 F3	Orchard Rd. SO31	13 E1	Pilning Clo. PO14	7 F5	Redhouse Park Gdns. PO12	21 E4
Netley Rd. PO14	13 G1	Ordnance Rd. PO12	24 B4	Pimpernel Clo. SO31	4 D6	Redlands La. PO14	8 A5
Neville Av. PO16	10 C5	Ordnance Row. PO1	25 F3	Pine Walk. SO31	5 E3	Redwood Dri. PO14	10 A3
Neville Ct. PO12	23 F1	Oriel Dri. PO14	13 G2	Pinetrees Clo. PO14	7 F5	Reeds Pl. PO12	21 G4
New Rd. PO16	8 B4	Orion Clo. PO14	15 H6	Pinewood, Brockhurst. PO13	21 E1	Reeds Rd. PO12	21 G3
New Rd, Sarisbury. SO31	4 D1	Orwell Cres. PO14	13 G1	Pinewood, Rowner. PO13	20 D1	Regent Pl. PO5	25 G6
New Rd, Warsash. SO31	12 C3	Osborn Cres. PO13	16 D4	Pinewood Clo. PO14	15 H4	Regents Gate. SO31	4 C4
Newbolt Rd. PO6	10 D3	Osborn Rd. PO16	8 B4	Pinks Hill. PO16	8 D4	Repton Clo. PO12	22 C2
		Osborn Rd South. PO16	8 B4	Pinto Clo. PO15	5 G2	

Richard Gro. PO12	21 F1
Richards Clo. SO31	5 F5
Richmond Pl. PO1	25 F3
Richmond Rd. PO13	19 F4
Richmond Rd, Privett. PO12	21 G6
Richmond Rise. PO16	10 B3
Ridgeway Clo. PO6	11 E2
Rimmers Ct, Broad St. PO1	25 E5
Riverside Av. PO16	8 D3
Roberts Rd. PO12	21 E4
Robins Clo. PO14	15 G5
Robins Meadow. PO14	13 G2
Robinson Ct. PO16	10 B3
Robinson Rd. PO14	18 D1
Rockingham Way. PO16	9 H5
Rodney Clo. PO13	20 C4
Rogate Gdns. PO16	10 B2
Rogers Clo. PO12	21 G4
Roman Gro. PO16	10 C6
Romford Rd. SO31	12 B3
Romsey Av. PO16	9 G5
Rookery Av. PO15	5 F2
Rooksw ay Gro. PO16	9 F5
Rosedale Clo. PO14	6 B5
Rosemary La. PO1	25 F3
Rosemary Walk. PO13	19 G4
Rosewood. PO13	20 D1
Ross Way. PO13	19 G4
Rossan Av. SO31	12 B3
Rothesay Rd. PO12	21 F3
Rothwell Clo. PO6	11 F3
Row Wood La. PO13	20 B1
Rowallen Av. PO13	20 B2
Rowan Clo. PO13	19 H5
Rowan Way. PO14	7 E6
Rowe Ash Way. SO31	5 E5
Rowland Rd. PO15	7 H4
Rowland Rd. PO6	10 D3
Rowner Clo. PO13	20 C1
Rowner La. PO13	20 C2
Rowner Rd. PO13	20 A1
Rudgwick Clo. PO16	9 G5
Runnymead. PO15	7 F2
Russell Clo. PO13	19 G4
Russell Pl. PO16	8 B4
Russell Rd. PO13	19 G5
Russell St. PO12	21 G4
Rydal Clo. PO6	11 G3
Rydal Rd. PO12	21 F2
Ryde Pl. PO13	19 H6
Ryecroft. PO14	5 G6
Sackville St. PO5	25 H4
St Andrews Rd. PO12	23 F2
St Annes Gro. PO14	7 H6
St Anns Cres. PO12	21 F4
St Catherines Way. PO16	9 E5
St Christopher Av. PO16	8 C3
St Christopher Gdns. PO13	17 E6
St Cuthberts Clo. SO31	5 F5
St Cuthberts La. SO31	5 F5
St Davids Rd. SO31	4 D6
St Edmunds Clo. PO14	13 G2
St Edwards Rd. PO12	23 F2
St Edwards Rd. PO5	25 H5
St Faiths Clo. PO12	23 E1
St Francis Clo. PO12	23 G5
St Georges Rd. PO1	25 F4
St Georges Rd. SO31	4 D6
St Georges Sq. PO1	25 F3
St Georges Way. PO1	25 F3
St Helena Way. PO16	10 B4
St Helens Rd. PO12	22 C3
St James's Rd. PO5	25 H4
St James's St. PO1	25 F3
St James's Way. PO16	10 B4
St Johns Clo. PO12	23 F1
St Johns Rd. SO31	5 F6
St Johns Sq. PO12	21 G5
St Joseph Clo. SO31	5 F5
St Judes Clo. PO5	25 H6
St Leonards Clo. PO15	6 B2
St Lukes Rd. PO12	21 F4
St Margarets La. PO14	6 B4
St Marks Clo. PO12	23 F4
St Marks Pl. PO12	23 F4
St Marks Rd. PO12	23 F4
St Marys Av. PO12	23 E3
St Marys Rd. PO14	15 G4
St Michaels Gro. PO14	7 H6
St Michaels Rd. SO31	5 E6
St Michaels Rd. PO1	25 G4
St Nicholas Rd. PO13	20 B2
St Nicholas St. PO1	25 F5
St Pauls Rd. PO5	25 G4
St Pauls Rd. SO31	4 D3
St Pauls Sq. PO5	25 G4
St Sebastian Cres. PO16	8 C3
St Simon Clo. SO31	5 F5

St Thomas a Becket Ct. PO1	25 F5
St Thomas Clo. PO16	8 C3
St Thomas's Ct. PO1	25 F5
St Thomas's Rd. PO12	21 G2
St Thomas's St. PO1	25 F5
St Tristan Clo. SO31	5 F6
St Valerie Rd. PO12	23 F3
St Vincent Rd. PO12	21 G4
Salerno Clo. PO12	21 F6
Salisbury Ter. PO13	19 G5
Salterns. PO16	8 C6
Salterns La. PO16	16 D1
Salterns Rd. PO16	18 C2
Sampan Clo. SO31	12 D2
Samson Rd. PO1	25 E2
Samson Clo. PO13	20 C3
San Diego Rd. PO12	21 G4
Sandcroft Clo. PO12	22 C3
Sandford Av. PO12	22 C2
Sandhill La. PO13	20 A3
Sandisplatt. PO14	7 E6
Sandown Clo. PO12	22 C3
Sandport Gro. PO16	10 A5
Sandringham Rd. PO14	7 E5
Sandy La. PO14	6 B6
Sandycroft. SO31	12 B2
Sanross Clo. PO14	18 C1
Savage Clo. PO13	20 D4
Savernake Clo. PO13	17 F6
Saville Clo. PO12	22 D2
Saville Gdns. PO16	8 A2
Saxon Clo. PO13	12 C1
Saxon Clo. PO16	10 B2
Scafell Av. PO14	7 F6
School Rd. PO12	21 C1
Schooner Way. SO31	12 C2
Scott Clo. PO14	15 G4
Scott Rd, Portsea. PO1	25 E2
Scott Rd, Southsea. PO1	25 F4
Sea Crest Rd. PO13	19 G5
Sea Horse Ct. PO12	24 C3
Sea Horse Walk. PO12	23 H1
Sea Kings. PO14	15 F5
Sea La. PO12	19 E2
Sea Mill Gdns. PO1	25 F3
Sea Mill Path. PO1	25 F3
Seabird Way. PO16	8 B6
Seafield Park Rd. PO14	18 C2
Seafield Rd. PO16	10 A5
Seagers Ct. PO1	25 E5
Seamead. PO14	19 E2
Seaton Clo. PO14	19 E1
Seaview Av. PO16	10 D3
Seaward Tower. PO12	24 C4
Seaway Gro. PO16	10 B5
Sedgefield Clo. PO6	10 D4
Sedgeley Gro. PO12	21 F2
Sedgewick Clo. PO13	20 B2
Segensworth East Ind Est.	
SO31	5 H4
Segensworth West Ind Est.	
SO31	6 A2
Selborne Gdns. PO12	21 F6
Selsey Av. PO12	21 F2
Serment. PO5	11 F5
Serpentine Rd. PO5	25 H6
Serpentine Rd. PO16	8 B3
Severn Clo. PO16	9 G5
Severn Clo. PO6	11 G2
Seymour Rd. PO13	19 H6
Shackleton Rd. PO13	20 C3
Shaftesbury Rd. PO11	23 G2
Shaftesbury Rd. PO5	25 H6
Shakespeare Mews. PO14	6 C5
Shalbourne Rd. PO12	21 F3
Shamrock Clo. PO12	24 B4
Shannon Clo. PO13	7 F4
Shannon Rd. PO14	15 F5
Sharpness Clo. PO14	7 F6
Shearwater Av. PO16	9 E5
Shearwater Clo. PO13	16 D6
Shellcroft. SO31	12 B2
Shelley Av. PO6	10 D3
Shenley Clo. PO15	7 E4
Shepards Clo. PO14	7 E6
Shepherds Purse Clo. SO31	4 D6
Sheridan Gdns. PO15	5 G1
Sherwin Walk. PO12	23 E3
Sherwood Gdns. SO31	4 C5
Sherwood Rd. PO12	21 F6
Shire Clo. PO15	5 F2
Shoot La. PO13	20 A2
Shore Rd. SO31	12 A2
Short Clo. PO14	18 C1
Short Row. PO1	25 F2
Shrubbery Clo. PO16	10 B5
Sibland Clo. PO14	7 F5
Silver Birch Av. PO14	7 G5

Silver St. PO5	25 G5
Simpson Clo. PO16	10 B3
Sissinghurst Rd. PC16	10 A5
Sixpenny Clo. PO14	13 F2
Skew Rd. PO17	10 B2
Skipper Way. PO13	19 G5
Skylark Way. PO13	19 G3
Slindon St. PO1	25 H3
Slingsby Clo. PO5	25 G5
Sloetree Clo. SO31	13 G1
Smeeton Rd. PO13	19 G4
Smith St. PO12	21 G5
Snap Dragon Clo. SO31	12 D1
Snape Clo. PO13	20 B2
Snowdon Dri. PO14	7 G6
Solent Dri. SO31	12 C4
Solent Rd. PO16	18 C1
Solent 2 Business Park. PO15	5 G2
Solent Vw. PO16	10 B3
Solent Way. PO12	22 D3
Somervell Clo. PO12	23 E4
Somervell Dri. PO16	8 A3
Sopwith Way. SO31	4 D1
Sorrel Clo. SO31	12 D1
South Clo. PO12	22 D3
South Cross St	24 C4
South Lodge. PO15	7 E5
South Normandy. PO1	25 F4
South Path. PO13	20 C5
South Pl. PO13	19 H6
South St. PO12	24 A5
South St. PO5	25 G5
South St. PO14	6 C6
South Ter. PO1	25 E2
Southampton Hill. PO14	6 C5
Southampton Rd. PO16	8 B4
Southampton Rd. SO31	5 G4
Southampton Rd. PO6	10 D4
Southampton Row. PO1	25 F3
Southcliff Rd. PO13	19 G4
Southcroft Rd. PO12	21 E5
Southmead Rd. PO15	7 F4
Southsea Ter. PO5	25 G6
Southway. PO13	17 E4
Southway. PO15	6 B3
Southways. PO14	15 H6
Southwick Av. PO16	10 D2
Southwick Ct. PO16	16 C1
Southwick Rd. PO6	11 G1
Southwood Gdns. SO31	4 D6
Sovereign Cres. PO14	13 F2
Sparrow Ct. PO13	19 H3
Spartan Clo. PO14	15 H3
Speedfields Park. PO13	16 C3
Speedwell Clo. SO31	12 D1
Spencer Ct. PO14	16 A6
Spencer Dri. PO13	19 H5
Spenser Clo. SO31	12 C3
Spicer St. PO1	25 H2
Spicewood. PO15	7 G3
Spithead Av. PO12	23 G5
Spring Ct. PO13	19 G5
Spring Garden La. PO12	24 B4
Spring Gdns. PO1	25 G3
Spring Rd. SO31	4 D3
Spring St. PO1	25 H2
Springcroft. PO13	16 D3
Springfield Way. PO14	19 E2
Spruce Clo. SO31	13 C2
Spruce Walk. PO13	19 G4
Spurlings Rd. PO. PO17	8 D1
Stable Clo. PO14	6 A4
Stalybridge Clo. SO31	5 E3
Standard Way. PO16	8 C2
Stanford Clo. PO6	11 H3
Stanhope Rd. PO1	25 H3
Stanley Clo. PO12	21 G1
Stanley Clo. PO15	7 G4
Staplers Reach. PO13	20 B1
Stares Clo. PO13	20 C3
Station App. PO1	25 E3
Station Hill. PO13	4 A1
Station Rd. PO12	21 E3
Station Rd, Bursledon. SO31	4 A1
Station Rd. PO16	10 C3
Station Rd, Swanwick. SO31	5 F3
Steel St. PO5	25 H3
Steep Clo. PO16	10 B2
Steeple Way. PO14	5 H6
Steinbeck Clo. PO15	5 G1
Stephen Rd. PO15	7 H4
Stephenson Clo. PO12	23 E4
Stirling Ct. PO15	7 G3
Stocker Rd. PO13	20 D1
Stoke Gdns. PO12	23 G2
Stoke Rd. PO12	23 F2
Stokes Bay Rd. PO12	22 C4
Stone La. PO12	23 F2

Stone St. PO5	25 G5
Stonecrop Clo. SO31	12 D1
Stoneleigh Clo. PO16	9 H6
Stoner Clo. PO13	16 D5
Stony La. PO1	25 E2
Stow Cres. PO15	7 F3
Stradbrook. PO13	20 B1
Strathmore Rd. PO12	24 A4
Stratton Clo. PO6	11 H3
Strawberry Hill. SO31	4 D5
Streamleaze. PO14	13 G1
Stroud Green La. PO14	15 H3
Stuart Clo. PO14	19 E1
Stubbington Grn. PO14	15 G5
Stubbington La. PO14	19 E1
Studland Rd. PO13	19 G5
Suffolk Dri. PO15	5 F2
Sullivan Clo. PO6	10 D4
Sumar Clo. PO14	15 H3
Summerfields. SO31	13 F1
Sun St. PO1	25 F3
Sunbeam Way. PO12	23 F3
Sunbury Ct. PO15	7 G2
Sunningdale Clo. PO13	20 C1
Sunningdale Rd. PO16	10 C4
Sunny Walk. PO1	25 E2
Surrey St. PO1	25 H3
Sussex Pl. PO5	25 H6
Sussex Rd. PO5	25 H6
Sussex Ter. PO5	25 H6
Swallow St. PO13	19 G3
Swallow Wood. PO16	8 B2
Swan Ct. PO13	16 D4
Swanage Rd. PO13	19 F4
Swancote. PO16	9 F5
Swanwick La. SO31	4 B1
Swanwick Shore Rd. SO31	4 B2
Sweet Hills Cres. PO15	5 F1
Swift Clo. PO13	19 G3
Swivelton La. PO17	9 G1
Sword Clo. PO12	22 D3
Sycamore Clo. PO13	20 D1
Sycamore Clo. PO14	13 G2
Sydney Rd. PO12	23 F1
Tait Pl. PO13	20 D1
Tallan Rd. PO14	13 F2
Tamar Clo. PO16	9 G5
Tamarisk Clo. PO14	19 E2
Tammys Turn. PO14	6 D6
Tanworth Pl. PO12	23 G2
Tanglewood. PO16	8 A2
Tanner La. PO14	16 A2
Tanyges Clo. PO14	15 H5
Tarius Clo. PO13	17 F5
Tarleton Rd. PO6	11 G3
Tatershall Cres. PO16	10 A5
Tawny Owl Clo. PO14	15 F3
Teal Clo. PO16	9 F6
Teal Walk. PO13	16 D5
Tedder Rd. PO13	17 F5
Teignmouth Rd. PO12	21 F3
Templemere. PO14	7 E6
Tennyson Gdns. PO16	8 A4
Tennyson Rd. PO13	19 F3
Tensing Clo. PO16	8 A2
Tern Walk. PO13	16 D5
Testcombe Rd. PO12	23 F3
Tewkesbury Av. PO12	21 G3
Tewkesbury Av. PO15	7 F2
Tewkesbury Clo. PO6	11 H3
Thames Dri. PO15	7 F1
Thamesmead Clo. PO12	21 F3
The Anchorage. PO12	24 A5
The Avenue. PO12	23 E4
The Avenue. PO14	7 E5
The Beachway. PO16	10 C6
The Brackens. SO31	13 F1
The Byres. PO14	15 G4
The Cascades. PO1	25 H2
The Causeway. PO16	9 E4
The Chantry. PO14	5 H6
The Chase, Privett. PO12	22 D2
The Chase,	
Titchfield Common. PO12	13 H1
The Chestnuts. PO6	11 F1
The Chine. PO13	20 D1
The Cloisters. PO15	7 E4
The Close. PO16	10 B4
The Close. PO14	6 B6
The Coppice. PO13	17 F6
The Copse. PO15	7 F1
The Croft. PO14	15 G4
The Crossway. PO16	10 A3
The Crossways. PO12	21 G4
The Curve. PO13	16 D5
The Dell. PO13	9 E4
The Downsway. PO16	10 B4
The Drive. PO16	8 A4

Street	Ref
The Drive. PO13	16 C6
The Fairway. PO16	10 B4
The Fairway. PO13	20 C1
The Firs. PO13	20 D1
The Florins. PO14	13 F2
The Gallops. PO14	6 A4
The Gannets. PO14	15 F5
The Gillies. PO16	8 A5
The Glade. PO15	7 F2
The Glades. SO31	5 E4
The Glebe. PO14	19 E1
The Glen. PO13	20 D1
The Greendale. PO15	7 F2
The Grove. PO14	15 F6
The Hard. PO1	25 E3
The Haven. PO12	23 F4
The Haven. SO31	5 G5
The Heights. PO16	8 D3
The Hillway. PO16	10 B3
The Hoe. PO13	20 D1
The Hurdles. PO14	6 A4
The Keep. PO16	10 C4
The Kingsway. PO16	10 B4
The Lane. PO12	23 F4
The Leaway. PO16	10 C4
The Leisure. PO13	17 F4
The Limes. PO13	17 F6
The Links. PO13	20 C1
The Linnets. PO16	9 F6
The Mallards. PO16	8 B2
The Maltings. PO16	8 D3
The Mary Rose St. PO1	25 H3
The Mead. PO13	16 D5
The Meadows. PO16	8 C2
The Mews. PO12	24 C4
The Mint. PO13	20 D1
The Nook. PO13	20 D1
The Oakes. PO14	15 F4
The Paddock. PO12	23 E2
The Paddock. PO14	15 G4
The Parade. PO1	25 E2
The Parkway. PO13	16 D6
The Pastures. PO14	5 G5
The Peregrines. PO16	9 F6
The Pines. PO16	9 G5
The Potteries. PO16	8 B3
The Precinct. PO12	24 C4
The Queens Mall. PO5	25 H4
The Queensway. PO16	10 A4
The Redan. PO12	23 G5
The Retreat. PO5	25 H6
The Ridgeway. PO16	9 E4
The Rosery. PO14	23 F4
The Scimitars. PO14	15 F5
The Seagulls. PO13	19 H6
The Shrubbery. PO12	21 F3
The Slipway. PO6	11 F5
The Spinney. PO16	9 F5
The Spinney. PO13	20 D1
The Spur. PO12	22 D4
The Square. PO12	21 H2
The Square. PO14	6 C5
The Tanners. PO32	13 G2
The Thicket. PO16	9 F4
The Thicket. PO13	20 D1
The Timbers. PO15	7 E5
The Vale. PO14	13 F2
The Waters. PO17	7 G1
Thetford Rd. PO12	21 E3
Thirlmere Clo. PO14	15 H4
Thomas St. PO1	25 H1
Thornbrake Rd. PO14	23 G2
Thornbury Clo. PO14	7 E5
Thorney Clo. PO14	7 F6
Thorngate Way. PO12	24 C4
Thorni Av. PO15	7 E2
Thornton Av. SO31	12 A2
Thornton Rd. PO12	21 H2
Three Tun Clo. PO1	25 F3
Tichbourne Way. PO13	20 D1
Tillingbourne. PO14	5 G6
Tintern Clo. PO6	11 E2
Tintern Rd. PO12	21 G6
Titchfield By-Pass. PO14	6 D5
Titchfield Hill. PO14	6 D5
Titchfield Park Rd. PO15	5 H6
Titchfield Rd. PO14	15 F1
Toby St. PO1	25 H2
Tollgate Rd. SO31	4 B1
Tonbridge St. PO5	25 H6
Tonnant Clo. PO14	19 E1
Topiary Gdns. SO31	5 F5
Tor Clo. PO16	9 E4
Toronto Pl. PO12	23 F1
Torquay Av. PO12	21 F2
Tortworth Clo. PO14	7 F5
Totland Rd. PO13	17 E6
Tower Clo. PO12	22 E3
Tower St. PO1	25 E5
*Town Quay, Broad St. PO1	25 E5
Trafalgar Ct. PO14	16 C1
Trafalgar Sq. PO12	21 G5
Trebourba Dri. PO12	23 E3
Trent Walk. PO16	9 G5
Trent Way. PO14	19 G5
Trevose Clo. PO13	17 E6
Trevose Way. PO14	13 G2
Triangle La. PO14	14 C4
Tribe Rd. PO12	21 G5
Trimaran Rd. SO31	12 C2
Trinity Clo. PO12	24 C4
Trinity Gdns. PO16	8 B4
Trinity Grn. PO12	24 C4
Trinity St. PO16	8 B3
Triumph Clo. PO15	7 F4
Truro Rd. PO6	11 E3
Tudor Clo. PO16	10 A2
Tudor Clo. PO13	20 D2
Tudor Ct. PO16	16 C1
Tukes Av. PO13	16 D4
Tulip Gdns. SO31	4 D6
Turner Av. PO13	20 D1
Turtle Clo. PO14	15 F4
Twiggs End Clo. SO31	4 D5
Twyford Dri. PO14	19 H4
Tynedale Ct. PO12	21 E2
Unicorn Rd. PO1	25 G2
Union St. PO16	8 C4
Union St. PO1	25 F3
Uplands Cres. PO16	8 B3
Upper Brook Dri. SO31	12 D1
Upper Cornaway La. PO16	10 A2
Upper Old St. PO14	15 F4
Upper St Michaels Gro. PO14	8 A6
Upper Spinney. SO31	12 B3
Upper Wharf. PO16	8 C5
Vadne Gdns. PO12	21 G4
Vale Gro. PO12	21 F3
Valentine Clo. PO15	7 E3
Valley Rise. SO31	4 D5
Valsheba Dri. PO14	18 C1
Vanstone Rd. PO13	20 D2
Varos Clo. PO12	21 G4
Vectis Rd. PO12	22 C3
Ventnor Rd. PO13	16 D5
Ventnor Way. PO16	9 E4
Verger Clo. PO14	5 H6
Vernon Clo. PO12	21 G5
Vernon Rd. PO12	21 G5
Veryan. PO14	7 G5
Vian Clo. PO13	17 E4
Vicarage La. PO14	15 G5
Victoria Clo. SO31	13 E2
Victoria Pl. PO12	23 F2
Victoria Rd. PO1	25 E1
Victoria Sq. PO13	19 F4
Victoria St. PO12	23 G1
Victory Rd. PO1	25 F3
Victory Rd. PO14	15 H6
Vikings Clo. PO14	15 F5
Village Rd. PO12	23 E4
Vincent Gro. PO16	10 B4
Vincent St. PO5	25 G4
Vine Clo. SO31	4 C6
Vineside. PO13	20 D1
Violet Av. PO14	15 F6
Virginia Park Rd. PO12	21 E4
Vixen Clo. PO14	15 F5
Vulcan Rd. PO1	25 E4
Wagtail Way. PO16	9 F5
Wakefield Av. PO16	7 H2
Walford Rd. PO6	11 G3
Walker Pl. PO13	20 D1
Wallington Ct. PO14	16 B1
Wallington Hill. PO16	8 C4
Wallington Shore Rd. PO16	8 D4
Wallington Way. PO16	8 C4
Wallisdean Av. PO14	7 H5
Walnut Dri. PO14	15 F6
Walpole Rd. PO12	24 B4
Waltham Clo. PO16	10 B2
Waltham St. PO5	25 G4
Walton Clo. PO12	23 F2
Walton Ct. PO15	7 F2
Walton Rd. PO12	23 F2
Wandesford Pl. PO12	21 G1
Warblington St. PO1	25 F4
Warnford Clo. PO12	21 F6
Warsash Gro. PO13	16 D6
Warsash Rd. SO31	12 C2
Warwick Clo. PO13	20 A6
Warwick Cres. PO5	25 H4
Washbrook Rd. PO6	11 H3
Waterloo Rd. PO12	23 G4
Waterloo St. PO5	25 H4
Watersedge Rd. PO6	11 F4
Waterside Gdns. PO16	8 D4
Waterside La. PO16	10 D6
Wavell Rd. PO13	17 F5
Waveney Clo. PO14	19 G4
Waverley Path. PO12	22 C2
Wayfarer Clo. SO31	12 D1
Webb Rd. PO16	10 C6
Wedgewood Clo. PO14	15 G6
Weevil La. PO12	24 B2
Welch Rd. PO12	21 G3
Wellington Gro. PO16	10 B5
Wellington St. PO5	25 H4
Wellow Gdns. PO14	13 G1
Wellsmoor. PO14	5 G6
Wessex Gdns. PO16	10 B4
West Bund Rd. PO6	11 F5
West Cliff Clo. PO13	19 G4
West Croft Rd. PO12	21 E5
West Downs Clo. PO16	8 B2
West St, Fareham. PO16	8 C5
West St, Portchester. PO16	10 A4
West St. PO1	25 E5
West St. PO14	6 B5
Westborn Rd. PO16	8 B4
Westbrook Clo. SO31	5 E3
Westbrook Rd. PO16	10 C5
Westbury Clo. PO6	11 G2
Westbury Rd. PO16	8 B4
Western Parade. PO5	25 G6
Western Rd. PO16	8 B5
Western Rd. PO6	11 H4
Western Way. PO16	8 A5
Western Way. PO14	22 C3
Westfield Av. PO14	7 H6
Westfield Rd. PO12	21 F6
Westgate. PO14	19 E1
Westland Gdns. PO12	23 E3
Westlands Gro. PO16	10 B5
Westley Gro. PO14	7 H5
Westminster Gdns. PO14	5 G6
Westway. PO15	6 B3
Westways. PO14	15 H6
Weyhill Clo. PO16	10 B2
Weymouth Av. PO12	21 F2
Whaddow Chase. PO14	15 F6
Wheatcroft Rd. PO13	19 G4
Wheatlands. PO14	5 G5
Wheeler Clo. PO12	21 G4
Whinchat Clo. PO15	7 E2
White Hart Alley. PO1	25 E5
White Hart La. PO16	10 A4
White Hart Rd. PO1	25 E5
White Lion Walk. PO12	23 H1
White Lodge Gdns. PO16	7 G2
White Swan Rd. PO1	25 G3
Whitebeam Clo. PO14	7 G5
Whitedell La. PO17	9 E1
Whitehart Rd. PO12	23 F2
Whitehaven. PO16	10 B4
Whiteley La. PO15	6 B2
Whiteley Way. PO15	5 H3
Whites Pl. PO12	21 G5
Whittle Av. SO31	5 G4
Whitworth Clo. PO12	23 F1
Whitworth Rd. PO12	21 G6
Wickham Rd. PO17	8 B1
Wickham St. PO1	25 E3
Wicor Mill La. PO16	10 A5
Wicor Path. PO16	10 A5
Widgeon Clo. PO12	21 H3
Widgeon Ct. PO16	9 F5
Widley Ct. PO14	16 C2
Wield Clo. SO31	5 E4
Wilberforce Rd. PO12	23 G4
Wilberforce Rd. PO5	25 H5
Wild Ridings. PO14	7 E6
Wild Rose Cres. SO31	12 C1
Wildern Clo. SO31	5 E5
Willersley Clo. PO6	11 H3
William Clo. PO14	19 E1
William Price Gdns. PO16	8 B4
Williams Clo. PO13	20 C3
Willis Rd, Gosport. PO12	24 B4
Willis Rd. PO1	25 H3
Willow Pl. PO12	21 H5
Willowherb Clo. SO31	12 C1
Willowtree Gdns. PO14	7 G5
Wilmott Clo. PO12	21 E5
Wilmott La. PO12	21 E5
Wilton Clo. PO12	21 F6
Wiltshire St. PO5	25 G4
Winchcombe Rd. PO6	11 G2
Windermere Av. PO14	15 H4
Windmill Gro. PO16	10 A5
Windsor Rd. PO12	21 G6
Windsor Rd. PO16	10 C5
Wingate Rd. PO12	21 F1
Winnards Pk. SO31	4 C5
Winnham Dri. PO16	9 G5
Winnington. PO15	7 F2
Winnington Clo. PO15	7 F2
Winston Churchill Av. PO5	25 G4
Winterbourne Rd. SO31	11 E2
Wises All. PO12	24 C4
Witherbed La. PO15	5 H5
Withies Rd. PO13	20 D2
Withington Clo. PO6	11 F3
Wood Clo. PO13	20 C1
Woodbourne Clo. PO15	7 F5
Woodcot La. PO13	16 C5
Woodhall Way. PO15	7 G2
Woodlands. PO16	8 D4
Woodlands Clo. SO31	4 D3
Woodley Rd. PO12	23 G2
Woodpath. PO5	25 H5
Woodpecker Copse. SO31	5 F6
Woodrush Cres. SO31	12 D1
Woodside. PO13	16 D3
Woodstock Clo. PO14	7 F5
Woodstock Rd. PO12	23 G2
Woodthorpe Gdns. SO31	5 E3
Woodvale. PO15	7 F4
Woodville Dri. PO5	25 G5
Woodward Clo. PO12	21 F6
Woofferton Rd. PO6	11 F2
Wootton Rd. PO13	19 H6
Wordsworth Av. PO6	10 D2
Workmans La. SO31	12 C5
Worsley Rd. PO5	25 H5
Worthing Av. PO12	21 F2
Wren Way. PO16	9 F6
Wych La. PO13	16 D4
Wycote Rd. PO13	16 D4
Wyndham Mews. PO1	25 F5
Wynton Way. PO15	7 E2
Yapton St. PO1	25 H3
Yarborough Rd. PO5	25 H5
Yarrow Way. SO31	12 D1
Yew Tree Ct. PO15	5 F2
Yew Tree Dri. PO15	5 F2
Yewside. PO13	17 F6
York Cres. PO13	20 A6
York Gdns. PO16	10 D5
York Pl. PO1	25 F2
York St. PO1	25 H3
Yorke St. PO5	25 G5
Young Bridge Ct. PO16	8 B6
Zetland Rd. PO12	23 F1